THE WEST POINT CANDIDATE BOOK

The Unofficial Guide to

HOW TO ★ HOW TO ★ HOW TO
PREPARE GET IN ★ SURVIVE

PLUS **ADVICE FOR PARENTS**

By Sue Ross
with Randy Lee

Silver Horn Books

Cover photos courtesy USMA.

First Edition 1990; Second Edition 2000; Third Edition 2009; Fourth Edition 2016

Although the authors and publisher have exhaustively researched all sources to ensure the accuracy and completeness of the information contained in this book, we assume no responsibility for errors, inaccuracies, omissions, or an inconsistency herein. Any slights of people or organizations are unintentional.

ISBN 978-0-9797943-7-7
Printed and bound in the United States of America

DISCLAIMER: This is an UNOFFICIAL publication and was not produced in conjunction with or by permission of the United States Military Academy, Department of the Army, or Department of Defense. Use of the information contained in this book does not guarantee admittance to the USMA. The views expressed in this book are solely those of the authors, and do not reflect the views of the United States Military Academy, Department of the Army, or the Department of Defense.

To All Who
Have Served

Table of Contents

A Word from the Authors

If you are reading this book, chances are you think you might want to go to West Point, or more officially, the United States Military Academy.

The first thing you should do is visit their web site and study it. You will learn the history of the institution, the kinds of courses you can take, the specifications of the physical and medical examinations that you must pass, and the names and backgrounds of all the professors. (The admissions web address is **www.westpoint.edu/admissions**.) The website will tell you what you have to do to get an appointment.

This book repeats some of what is on the web site, and often refers you to specific pages of the web site for more details. Mainly, however, this is a "how to" book.

It will tell you how to prepare for the Academy.

One chapter, which is probably the most important one in the book, tells you how to prepare mentally — how to ensure you approach the challenges of West Point with the right attitude, motives, and perspective. Other chapters tell you how to prepare academically, physically, and in other important ways. Some of the preparation advice is intended to help you get into West Point; some is designed to help equip you to succeed once you get there.

This book will also give you valuable advice on how to get into the Academy.

The admissions process is very complex. Many of your peers will eliminate themselves simply because they fail to complete all the required steps. If you are dedicated enough to see the process through, you have already separated yourself from much of the competition.

The second section describes all the admissions procedures. One chapter describes how to get a congressional nomination and some of the pitfalls of that process. Other chapters give you guidelines on how to conduct yourself during interviews, and how you might be able to get into the Academy by alternate routes if you are now unqualified or have failed to get in by the regular procedures.

The book also tells you how to survive when you get to the Academy, with proven advice acquired through interviews with hundreds of cadets, graduates, professors, and staff officers — those who know what works and what doesn't.

You learn about the first year, which from a physical and psychological standpoint, is the hardest. Cadets will tell you what you must do to survive, with special advice for intercollegiate athletes, women and others who will be in the minority at the Academy.

We hope this book will help if you are not sure whether you should apply to West Point, by letting you see what a cadet's life is like. We hope you will be honest about whether you belong there. Not everyone does.

If you do decide to go, and receive an appointment, we recommend that you reread the chapters in this third section very carefully.

The final chapter is for parents. It is a compendium of advice gleaned from interviews with a wide variety of parents from around the United States. The advice comes from parents who have had sons and daughters at the Academy and who believe some of the hard lessons they learned should be shared. This chapter also includes cadets' advice for parents on how to — and how not to — support them.

After you read this book, take an honest look at yourself and see if you have the one thing you need most: a burning desire to become a West Point cadet. If you are easily discouraged or don't feel that burning desire, take some friendly advice and start looking into other good schools such as Princeton or Oklahoma State — and save yourself lots of headaches.

A final word: Thousands upon thousands of young men and women have made it into the United State Military Academy and managed to graduate. Practically all of them will tell you that it was one of the greatest experiences of their life — that it made them into something they would never have become without that experience. If you really want to "be all that you can be," go for it!

— *SCR & RHL*

THE INSTITUTION

CHAPTER 1
The Academic Institution

The United States Military Academy, commonly known as West Point, is a beautiful and historic site located on the Hudson River, about 60 miles north of New York City.

The buildings are clustered on a high bluff on the west side of the river. This is the site where General George Washington had a fort built during the Revolutionary War to guard the Hudson River and keep British ships and troops from moving upstream. Washington feared that if the British controlled the river, they would divide the young nation and conquer each half separately.

West Point is located on the banks of the Hudson River.   *United States Military Academy*

General Washington also had a heavy chain stretched across the river as a barrier against ships. This was a monumental task because the chain weighed 150 tons and had to be floated into place each spring and removed each autumn before the river froze.

The combination of the fort and the chain was successful, and no British ship managed to pass during the war. However, the outcome might have been different had some colonists not stopped and searched a man coming downstream from the fort. They discovered a paper hidden in his shoe, a proposal from the commander of West Point for selling the plans of the fortifications to the British. The man carrying the proposal was hanged as a spy. The commander of West Point, General Benedict Arnold, escaped to Great Britain but lived the rest of his life branded as a traitor, even by the British.

In 1802, Congress established the U.S. Military Academy on the site where the fort stood. The mission of the Academy was to train officers who would also be engineers for the Army — a goal George Washington had long advocated because of the desperate shortage of engineers during the war.

West Point became the first military and engineering school in the United States. However, its academic standards for the first fifteen years were very loose and the quality of its graduates was questionable.

The academic program improved after 1817, when Colonel Sylvanus Thayer became Superintendent of the Academy and strengthened the academic standards. Included in his program were two new requirements: (1) all students, called cadets, will recite every day in every class, and (2) no class will contain more than 15 cadets. The small class size enabled instructors to quiz each cadet and hold each one accountable for every assignment. Thayer served as superintendent for 16 years. During his tenure the quality of education at the Academy improved greatly, and soon it was turning out the high quality engineers the young, growing nation badly needed.

Throughout the years, West Point has trained many of America's top military leaders. During the Civil War, those included Union Generals Grant, Sherman, Sheridan and Meade, and Confederate Generals Lee, Johnston, Jackson, Bragg and Longstreet. The President of the Confederate States, Jefferson Davis, was also a graduate. Of the 60 major battles fought in that war, West Pointers commanded both sides during 55 of them, and in the other five battles there was a West Point graduate commanding either the Union or the Confederate forces. After the war, West Point graduates helped settle the western frontier.

During World War I, the general commanding the American forces, John J. Pershing, was a West Pointer. Also in that war, Colonel Douglas MacArthur, Class of 1903, was decorated nine times for extraordinary heroism while fighting in France.

During World War II, West Point again provided most of the

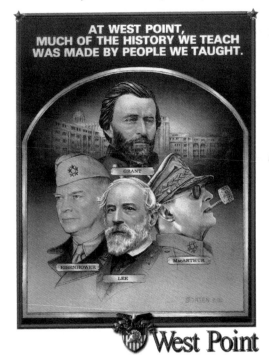

AT WEST POINT, MUCH OF THE HISTORY WE TEACH WAS MADE BY PEOPLE WE TAUGHT.

West Point

If you attend West Point, you become part of history.
United States Military Academy

key leaders: Generals Eisenhower, Patton, Bradley and Clark in the European theatre; Generals MacArthur, Stillwell and Wainwright in the Pacific; and General "Hap" Arnold in Washington who led the Army Air Force.

Two of those wartime leaders went on to become U.S. Presidents. General Grant served two terms, from 1869 to 1877. General Eisenhower also served two terms, from 1953 to 1961.

Why the history lesson? A popular saying at West Point goes, "The history we teach was made by the people we taught." If you are considering attending the Military Academy, you will be expected to know and appreciate its legacy.

Perhaps more importantly, the saying implies an obligation: You need to think of yourself as part of the next generation of leaders. In the twenty-first century, West Pointers are leading the war on terrorism, and will help write the next chapter of American military history. Future graduates will no doubt have the same heavy responsibility.

THE ACADEMIC PROGRAM

Despite the strong connection with the past, the mission of West Point today is changing to meet the broader needs of our highly technical, highly mobile Army. Today's Army needs officers with a broad education and the ability and desire to keep on learning throughout their professional careers.

All cadets take courses that will enable them to master the technological challenges of the Army — courses such as calculus, chemistry, computer science, and physics. But they also study political science, foreign language and culture, history, economics, literature and writing, and geography — subjects that will give them the skills and intellectual breadth to grow and function in (and out of) the Army.

At the heart of West Point's curriculum is the core — 26 courses across a broad field of study that provide a common foundation for every graduate. West Point offers 36 academic majors, including majors in regional studies, kinesiology, and environmental engineering, reflecting the environment where today's new officers will serve.

How good is the academic program at West Point? It was recently named Top Public College by *US News and World Report*. *The Princeton Review*'s annual college guide ranked West Point in its "Top 10" in 13 categories and "Top 20" in four others, including #1 in "Most Accessible Professors," #2 in "Best Health Services," and #3 in both "Best College Library" and "Most Politically Active Students." Forbes Magazine ranked West Point #11 out of 650 colleges, and #1 for Top Public College. (2015 Numbers)

Another measure of success is graduate scholarships. West Point has had 91 Rhodes Scholars since 1923, the fifth highest number in the nation — and a significant accomplishment, considering thousands of American college students compete for just 32 Rhodes Scholarships each year. West Point graduates have also received a large number of Truman and Marshall scholarships and Fulbright grants.

By these measures, one can see that West Point is widely respected as an academic institution. But what makes it so good?

At the top of the list is the attitude of the professors. The faculty is made up of approximately 80% military officers, many of whom have recent combat experience along with their academic degrees. The other 20% are civilians, many of whom have years of teaching experience and impressive academic credentials.

Regardless of their backgrounds, they share a dedication to their academic discipline and to teaching — or more accurately, a dedication to their students' learning. Teaching methods have evolved, but cadets can still expect small class sizes and frequent graded exercises that ensure preparation and understanding.

Instructors will also make themselves available for "Additional Instruction,"

West Point professors are known for their dedication to cadets.
United States Military Academy

meeting struggling cadets in their offices or the library to go over difficult material. As the vice dean explains, "We're not working under an attrition model. If we accept a cadet, we expect him or her to succeed. Our mission is to be accessible to cadets." While West Point professors publish papers and conduct meaningful research, their primary mission is teaching cadets. This explains the recognition for "most accessible professors" mentioned above.

Despite this extra help, not every cadet will be able to meet the academic challenges of West Point. Each year, a small number will be disenrolled for failing to meet academic standards. But they will leave knowing that the institution did all it could to help them succeed. As one upperclass cadet explained, "Everyone here wants to help you succeed."

In summary, while West Point is unmistakably a military school with the mission of creating U.S. Army officers, it will provide you with an education as good as or better than any in the country. Yet there is one other distinct difference: At many large civilian universities, you will probably be a faceless body in a large lecture hall, a number on a roster, someone the professor has probably never met. At the Academy, you will receive the personal attention of a dedicated faculty who knows your strengths and weaknesses, a faculty committed to your learning and available to help you when you stumble. In the words of a math professor, "If you want to succeed, if you're willing to make the sacrifices, the help is there for you."

That's hard to beat. And it's free, right? Well, in the literal sense, yes. But as any cadet or graduate will tell you, it isn't that simple. The next chapter will begin to explain why.

CHAPTER 2

The Military Institution

West Point is a first-class college, and a West Point degree will prepare you well for any career, whether in uniform, government, academia, or business.

But make no mistake: West Point is a military school. For this reason, the life of the cadet is nothing like the life of a student in a civilian college. If the traditional college experience is what you're after, the freedom and fun you've been hearing about from your older siblings and friends, best look elsewhere.

The military training during the first year is the hardest. It begins around the first of July, and consists of an initial six-week indoctrination period, officially called Cadet Basic Training (CBT), sometimes known as "Beast Barracks," or just "Beast."

West Point is much more than a college. You will also learn to be a Soldier. *United States Military Academy*

CBT has a number of purposes. First is to teach the new cadets[1] the traditions, courtesies and basic knowledge of the Army in general and West Point in particular.

Second is to train the new cadets the way a new soldier in the Army would be trained.

[1]New cadet is the name used until after CBT and acceptance into the Corps of Cadets. Then they become fourth classmen or "plebes." Sophomore-year cadets are third classmen or "yearlings" (sometimes called "yucs"), while junior-year cadets are second classmen or "cows," and seniors are first classmen or "firsties."

This includes training them to follow orders instantly and without question, teaching them basic combat skills, and pushing them through a rigorous period of physical development.

Third is to put the new cadets in a very demanding environment where they will be forced to learn how to manage their time efficiently and use teamwork to achieve the goals set for them. The demanding environment teaches self-discipline, and the teamwork training teaches the new cadets to subordinate their individual desires and work for the betterment of the group. This, in turn, develops the group pride that is essential for any effective military unit.

CBT is designed to integrate new cadets into West Point and Army life, and teach them what it is like to be a follower — the idea being that they will make better officers and leaders when they know what it is like to be a new soldier.

Cadet Basic Training is simply the first and most concentrated segment of an overall four-year leadership development program, a program discussed in extensive detail in following chapters. The military training during the academic year is not as concentrated as during CBT; however, with a heavy load of demanding classwork, and the additional pressure of mandatory intramural athletics (required of all cadets who do not play intercollegiate sports), the pressure of the leadership development program continues to be a heavy source of stress throughout the academic year.

The cadets say that every year there are new cadets who report to West Point believing that once the six weeks of Beast are over, they are relatively free to become normal college students. Do not be so naïve!

According to many cadets, the end of CBT and the beginning of the academic year is the hardest part of the year. They point out that during CBT, the new cadets outnumber the upperclassmen who are giving them the training. But, with the beginning of the academic year and the return of the whole Corps of Cadets, the plebes are outnumbered almost three to one — with almost every upperclassman eager to bring his or her own talents to the job of plebe military development. Further, during CBT, new cadets are told exactly what to do and when to do it, and are almost always in a group of their peers. Once the school year begins, plebes must figure out how to juggle multiple tasks, and many find that the little bit of freedom they now have can be a dangerous temptation.

The candidate also should put the leadership development program into perspective. It is not only a system to develop plebes; the system

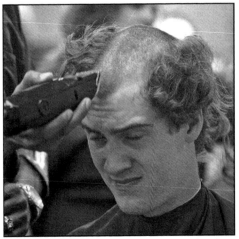

Some days, you may wonder what happened to the old you.   *United States Military Academy*

also provides an environment for the upperclassmen to work on their own leadership skills.

It is a goal of West Point to turn out officers with the leadership skills needed to function in the Army immediately after graduation. They learn some leadership skills during various summer training experiences, which include short stints in the real Army. But their main experience comes from within the institution through the leadership responsibilities they assume as upperclassmen.

Nearly every cadet will spend at least one dark night wondering what their buddies from high school are doing, what life is like at State U, what they are missing while shining shoes and studying "knowledge," the seemingly endless list of facts, quotes, and current events all plebes must memorize. Most will question, at least for a moment, why they are enduring the intense, rugged, four-year experience of the Academy.

Is it worth it? Consider the following: First, each graduate receives a Bachelor of Science Degree from one of the finest colleges in the country. Second, each graduate is awarded a commission in the Army as a second lieutenant. Thus, unlike civilian colleges, West Point gives its graduates a job guarantee. Third, they will have bonded with friends who will be their friends for life — friends who will literally put their lives on the line for one another. And graduates will have experienced great personal growth — growth far beyond what graduates at civilian institutions will experience.

What kinds of growth? Read what the graduates in the next chapter have to say.

CHAPTER 3

Graduates Speak: What the Academy Did for Me

Every college has its proud alumni, graduates who wear the school sweatshirts on weekends and put their alma mater's bumper stickers on their cars. They root for the football team and return for class reunions. They might brag about their sports teams or reminisce about the fun they had in their sororities and fraternities.

You probably won't hear many West Point grads bragging about the football team or the great parties they had on weekends. You probably won't hear them gloating that they got a great education for free, even though they did.

In most cases, you will hear Academy graduates talk about being part of a special kind of team. They talk about the leadership lessons they learned, the sometimes-painful road to self-discovery and greater strength of character. And they will all till you their lives would not be the same if they had gone to school somewhere else. Why? Read their stories and find out.

Mike Miles, Class of 1978

Raised in an Army family, Mike Miles wanted to go to West Point since elementary school. He graduated 8th in his class and became an Infantry officer and Ranger. After fulfilling his active duty commitment, he earned advanced degrees from UC Berkeley and Columbia, focusing on Soviet studies and international affairs. He became a Foreign Service Officer and served in embassies in Poland and Russia. He then began a third career in public service as a high school teacher, principal, and superintendent. Mr. Miles now applies his expertise with his firm Third Future, helping turn around struggling schools.

My dad was an Army NCO [non-commissioned officer], and he used to inspect the room I shared with my two brothers, even checking the top of the door for dust. So I knew the traditions; I knew what to expect. I knew West Point would be tough, but being mentally prepared was helpful. I remember the first inspection, when the upperclassmen ran his white glove over the top of the door. He was just sure he'd find dust, but I'd cleaned it.

I never felt like quitting, even though it was hard, and there was a lot of

Miles in a classroom with students. *Courtesy Mike Miles*

studying. I knew it was what I wanted to do. I was always a good student, and academically I felt pretty well prepared.

The friendships you form there are key. If I needed any emotional support, I got it from the other cadets. When you're in a hard situation like that, you develop strong bonds. I was also lucky to have great roommates.

My first assignment was in Fort Lewis, Washington, where I was able to join a Ranger battalion. After five years in the Army, I decided I wanted to be involved in policy-making, not just policy execution. So I went back to school for five years, studying Slavic languages and literature, the Soviet Union, international affairs and political science. I had a number of good scholarships, and my choice of good schools. The two years of Russian I had learned at West Point allowed me to enter a highly-selective program at Berkeley and study abroad in Leningrad.

I then got a paid internship with the State Department, working at the Bureau of Intelligence and Research and then the Soviet desk. I passed the Foreign Service exam and went to Warsaw, Poland, and I was in the Moscow embassy at the end of the Cold War — very interesting times.

After starting a family abroad, my wife and I decided to come home to Colorado. I feel that few things are as important as public education, for the strength of our democracy. So I found myself teaching civics in the same high school classroom where I had been a student.

Leadership is the most important, broadest lesson I took from West Point — the lessons I learned there helped in every single job I had. It allowed me to move up faster than I ever would have otherwise. I was selected to be the special assistant to the Ambassador to the Soviet Union. I became a principal without being an assistant principal first.

I learned that leadership is more than being directive. West Point taught me how to motivate people, how to listen to people and tap their strengths, and how to work as a team. It taught me to be self-aware and self-disciplined, which are required before you can lead others. Those lessons might not be taught in any class, they might not be graded, but they're the most important.

The second biggest lesson might be counter-intuitive, because the Academy is so regimented, but West Point expanded my world view immensely. I gained a greater appreciation for different approaches to problems, issues, and social concerns. I learned to think beyond the status quo.

A West Point education is more than just engineering; you get liberal arts too — language, history, and literature — all taught in a way that teaches critical thinking. I carried that with me all through my life. My favorite book is Cyrano de Bergerac, which I first read at West Point. He's a man of thought and a man of action, a poet as well as a fighter.

If you're considering West Point, be sure about the long term commitment — four years at the Academy plus five years in the Army, and even beyond that. They're training world leaders, for war, but also leaders to deal with problems beyond the Army. If you're not committed to leadership and solving problems, it's probably not worth the investment. Even though I've had three very different careers, above all I consider myself a public servant — that's what I do.

Lieutenant General (retired) Michael Linnington, Class of 1980

After attending four years of high school at Valley Forge Military Academy in Wayne, PA, LTG Linnington received his appointment to West Point. He graduated from West Point in 1980, as an Infantry officer. He earned a Master's Degree in Applied Mathematics from Rensselaer Polytechnic Institute and taught math at the U.S. Military Academy. He commanded the 3rd Brigade, 101st Airborne Division in Kandahar, Afghanistan and then in Iraq. He also served as Assistant Commandant and Deputy Commanding General at the U.S. Army Infantry Center at Fort Benning, Georgia. In May of 2008, General Linnington became Commandant of Cadets at West Point. Linnington concluded his military career as the Commanding General of the Army's Military District of Washington, and as Military Deputy to the Under Secretary of Defense (Personnel and Readiness). LTG Linnington's wife, Brenda, is a 1981 West Point graduate; their son, Michael, is a 2005 graduate of West Point. He is now CEO of the Wounded Warrior Project.

The second oldest of six boys, I learned early the lessons of teamwork and leadership. My parents were extremely hard working and not wealthy, yet managed to send us to Valley Forge Military Academy. On partial scholarship, I worked in the student lunchroom and at the student store. My parents' example stayed with me, and I worked hard at my jobs and on my academics. The thought of going to West Point was a natural one, and I was excited to receive one of two appointments from my high school.

Linnington mentoring West Point Cadets when he was Commandant of Cadets. *United States Military Academy*

Discipline was something I had grown up with both at home and in school, so I adapted easily to Academy life. I have to admit, though, I was a bit rebellious, given my 18 previous years of regimentation, and I "bucked the system" on occasion and was not the best cadet. I received many demerits and walked my share of punishment tours; yet I still felt at home, and enjoyed the camaraderie that comes with being a member of a very special team. Most of my closest friends today are my West Point classmates: a band of brothers and sisters I'll know for the rest of my life. Although I briefly considered leaving West Point to join my older brother in our family real estate business, I knew I was where I needed to be. I graduated in the middle of my class and had the distinction of being a century man[1]. Who would have thought I'd end up as the Commandant of Cadets many years later!

[1] A "century man" is a cadet who has marched 100 or more punishment tours, a monotonous and time-wasting punishment for minor disciplinary infractions.

The Academy taught me the basic military and life skills necessary to be a successful Army officer. My time at West Point taught me the importance of hard work, discipline, and sharing adversity with those you lead. I learned the values of integrity and teamwork, and the importance of strong relationships, both with peers, subordinates, and seniors. And I grew to understand the impact on one's character by living under the Honor Code.

The days at West Point are really full. You have to plan your days before they begin and use every minute effectively, or you'll invariably get behind. I think good time management skills and remaining disciplined help in living a life of integrity and internalizing the tenets of the Cadet Honor Code. Getting behind through poor time management skills often tempts cadets to take shortcuts that not only hurt them at West Point, but ultimately hurt them down the road in the military, and in life as well.

I tried my best to keep a positive attitude while at West Point, despite the challenges of being a cadet. That's an important part of being successful. Take the training seriously, but don't take yourself too seriously. Keep a sense of perspective and a good sense of humor. It's going to be a long road to reach your goals, so remember you can't sweat the small stuff along the way. I've always believed that nothing that's worthwhile in life comes easily.

When life as a cadet gets hard, and the demands seem overwhelming, remember that if you were given an appointment, you definitely have the potential to succeed. Many cadets question their abilities, because they are accustomed to being at the top of their class in high school and now they may be in the middle or bottom. It doesn't matter; everyone cadet something to contribute and possesses great potential for the future.

The leadership skills the Academy teaches you will make you successful in the Army or whatever you do in life. I found great opportunities to grow as a leader, from being put in charge as a group leader during New Cadet Training during an obstacle course all the way up to being a platoon leader during my final academic semester. Even in the classroom, there are leadership opportunities. You can get a great education anywhere if you're willing to work. But here you also get the world's best leadership development.

West Point is not for everyone. The environment is stressful: high expectations, physical demands, time-management demands, knowledge requirements, and living a military lifestyle are all adjustments in your first year. If you're considering attending West Point because your parents want you to, or any other reasons other than YOU truly want to attend (and serve your country in the Army after graduation), you'll have a very hard time, and I recommend you decide on a college experience someplace else. If you accept an appointment, resolve to work hard and make it through to graduation.

So my advice to candidates is to decide if you want to reach your full potential. If so, go to West Point! Realize you are accepting a challenge most Americans won't ever get the opportunity to achieve. You're going to have to work very hard, but you won't be alone. West Point has a stellar group of staff and faculty to help you reach your goals, and classmates that will be there for you, both as a cadet and after.

I can honestly say that everything good in my adult life can be attributed to West Point. I met my wife of 34 years at West Point; I have lifelong friendships established at West Point; and I received a strong professional foundation for service to my country that will remain with me for the rest of my life. Army Strong!

Joseph M. DePinto, Class of 1986

Joe DePinto grew up playing competitive sports and as a cadet at West Point, he played intercollegiate ice hockey for two years and graduated with a bachelor's degree in math, science and engineering management. Joe also has an MBA from the Kellogg School at Northwestern University. He served in the U.S. Army for five years and was a Field Artillery officer. After leaving the military, he worked at a number of major corporations, including PepsiCo and was President of Game Stop, Corp. Since 2005, he has been President and CEO of 7-Eleven, Inc. His son John graduated from West Point in the class of 2012.

My initial exposure to West Point was during east coast college visits with my junior ice hockey team. From the first time on the Academy grounds, I knew it was a place I'd like to attend. The cadets were impressive and seemed larger than life. I was interested in playing hockey in college, and knew the academics at West Point would be first rate. Additionally, the idea of serving my country in the military was appealing. Based on these feelings, I decided to pursue West Point.

Joe DePinto uses what he learned at West Point to lead an international corporation. *Courtesy Joe DePinto*

Beast Barracks was a lot tougher than I expected. It was intense, and there was a great amount of stress. There never seemed to be enough time to do what was on the schedule each day. Overall, I did well with the military training and the physical part of Cadet Basic Training, but wish I'd prepared better for all the running that occurred those first several weeks.

When the academic year started, I struggled with the workload and intensity of my classes. The Academy is good at giving you too much to do with limited time. So as in Beast, prioritization was important and properly managing homework each night imperative. I learned strong time management skills, taking advantage of open time throughout the day to balance the workload.

From a leadership perspective, I believe there is no better institution. Everything you do at West Point is focused on leadership. I learned a great deal from the Behavioral Science and Leadership classes. As part of West Point's training, cadets are put in positions where they are able to apply what they've learned. For me it really was a leadership training lab. You're also surrounded by military officers who become great coaches and mentors. I thought the Academy's people and infrastructure excelled at delivering leadership lessons. Collectively they work together to train cadets to be strong leaders and problem solvers.

They also teach that completing the mission and taking care of soldiers is what the military is all about.

What I enjoyed most about being in the Army was the sense of mission, the esprit de corps and camaraderie, being able to lead great soldiers, and the focus on team. The Army is all about people and teamwork. Some of this culture is seen in the corporate world, but it is difficult to truly replicate the sense of mission, teamwork and tight bonds that develop among those in the military.

As a CEO, I always approach the business with the same problem solving, can-do attitude learned at West Point, knowing there's a solution to any problem, and constantly searching for new opportunities to grow our business. I see many of these traits in the non-commissioned officers and junior officers we hire today at 7-Eleven. They know how to get things done and are good at making decisions. They're experienced, logical thinkers who work very well under stress and believe in teamwork.

From a people perspective, the Academy also taught me emotional intelligence, and gave me a strong understanding of the importance in developing relationships. Listening to understand those around you, asking clarifying questions, being prompt, courteous, respecting protocol, and doing what you say you're going to do. These traits are valued by all cultures and countries, and I follow these principles today leading a global business.

My advice to candidates considering West Point is to visit. Spend time with cadets in the barracks and in the classroom. Visit the coach and team if you're an athlete. Talk with cadets; ask questions to determine what life is really like at West Point. Be sure serving in the Army has appeal to you; and if not don't even consider the Academy. Know that there's a good chance you may see armed combat, even if you only serve for your initial commitment.

As a plebe, the most important thing is to be a great teammate. Always think in terms of being part of the team. Look out for your classmates. Mine saved me many times, and I always tried to return the favor. That's the key to success at the Academy. Everyone has strengths and weaknesses, so work together, help each other out and graduate.

Remember there are mentors all around you who've already been in your shoes. They can talk through things with you when you're having tough times. There were always upperclassmen and officers willing to talk with me when I was struggling. I never considered quitting West Point because of the bond I had with other cadets. I felt commitment to the team. That's the true test of team — when you're doing it because of mutual accountability, not for yourself. Even today, most of my best friends are Academy classmates.

Colonel (retired) Greg Gadson, Class of 1989

Greg Gadson grew up in Chesapeake, Virginia, and was recruited by a football coach. After attending USMA Prep School, he played varsity football for four years at West Point. After graduation, he married a classmate, Kim, and entered the Field Artillery. He saw combat in Iraq in 1991, Bosnia, Afghanistan, and then again as a battalion commander in Iraq in 2007. In May of 2007, Colonel Gadson was injured by a roadside bomb and lost both legs. His last active duty assignment was garrison commander of Fort Belvoir, Virginia. He has acted in the movie Battleship and the TV series The Inspectors, and is a frequent public speaker. He is currently managing partner of Patriot Strategies, LLC, a government services company. He also wears a Giants Super Bowl ring, as you will read about below.

I decided to go to West Point because it was my only opportunity to play Division I football. I had no experience with the military, and I didn't honestly understand what West Point was. I didn't start the application process until February of my senior year, which is too late. I also needed some academic strengthening, so I went to prep school.

Prep school gave me another year to mature, understand what I was getting into, and grow physically. It turned out to be very good for me because I think in the end the adjustment at West Point was insignificant, not that big a deal. In CBT, I understood the game, so most of the time I was smiling underneath.

My plebe year, I didn't feel like academics were that difficult, in large part because of the prep school. I ended up making varsity plebe year and lettering, and I think because the fourth class system wasn't that big of a deal for me, I was able to really focus

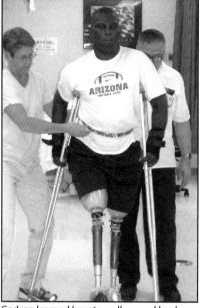

Gadson learned how to walk — and lead — on two prosthetic legs.   *Courtesy Greg Gadson*

on academics and football. My first year I did pretty well academically, which I think gave me a false sense of how easy it was going to be.

The level of scrutiny that I was exposed to at football practice was the biggest shocker to me. That sense of pressure, the feeling that I couldn't let up for a single play, was very significant.

I got into some academic trouble my sophomore year. I chose Arabic for a foreign language, because I thought it was going to be relevant in the future. Since there were so few cadets taking Arabic, I took it plebe year and pushed chemistry back to yearling year. They told me, "You have 22 credit hours. You ought to save chemistry for summer school." Being a man of pride, I said, "I can handle it." I had moved up in the depth chart in football, and I had third semester calculus, third semester Arabic, economics, physics, chemistry…it was a nightmare. I not only ended up failing calculus but also wrecked my GPA, and spent the rest of my career correcting that semester.

So I had to go to summer school and had a really bad GPA. But like any thing that's difficult, you learn from it. I went to summer school the following summer for English, then had to go to Beast Barracks [as cadre], then summer physical training. I hadn't left the Academy all year, so I went to the coach and asked for a few days off. I think that's the only thing I ever asked for. I went home, and bought my wife's engagement ring. Talk about pressure? I thought, "I can't screw this up. I have to graduate on time." I think I work better under pressure! We got married three days after graduation.

The day I was injured in Iraq, I was heading back to my headquarters from a memorial service, and I saw a big flash and knew exactly what had happened. I remember lying there knowing I was in bad shape. I was medevac'd to a Baghdad hospital, then to Walter Reed. Over the next two weeks, they took my left leg to save my life. When I found out my right leg wasn't going to work again, and I might end up having to have it amputated later anyway, my wife and I made the decision to have them take it also. I was really tired of all the surgery and wanted to get on with it. Within a month and a half of the attack, I started the process of getting the prosthetic.

My classmate and football teammate Mike Sullivan, like many in the West Point family, came by to visit me in the hospital. He's one of the New York Giants coaches, and at the time, the Giants were 0 and 2 and really struggling. So Mike thought I could help them. I talked to the team much like I would talk to my soldiers. I talked to them about doing your best. As much as outside world scrutinizes you, remember you're only playing for yourselves, for each other. All the things we do deployed, fighting for our country, they're all important. But at the end of the day, you're really fighting for each other. I ended up going to the playoffs and the Super Bowl with them.

I've enjoyed being in the Army. I'm a soldier. I still enjoy it, but at the same time there are days that are tough. I asked to go to graduate school because I was making decent progress in physical therapy, and wanted something to challenge myself. If it didn't work out, it wouldn't hurt anybody who was depending on me to do something.

What I took from my time at West Point starts with the professional ethic — understanding that we are in something that has high stakes. We don't have a large margin of error. That's what ought to motivate you to get up every day: that you may be called to serve your country, and you ought to do everything you can to be successful.

It's really about taking care of your people. You have the responsibility to train them and take care of them, so you can do what you're asked to when the time comes. I think of myself as a coach. You can be tough at times, but at the same time you have to be compassionate, and have fun.

The biggest thing that stands out after what happened to me is the concentric circles of support: The Army family, the West Point family, my football family, all my friends, then my closest friends, and at the center my family. There's not a lot of distance between those circles. West Point shows you that when you put so much into something together, so much sacrifice, a lot of time can go by since you saw someone, but the bonds will last a lifetime. I'm so impressed by the support from the Army and West Point, how they rallied around me to help me and my family get through this.

My advice to plebes is just take one day at a time. It's very easy to look at it as an insurmountable task. It can seem overwhelming. Recovering from this IED attack seemed overwhelming at times. You just go back to what got you through the difficult times in the past…taking it one day at a time.

Keep your eye on the prize. The goal is to graduate. Try to do your best every day. And learn from your experiences.

Colonel (retired) Kristin Baker, Class of 1990

Colonel Baker grew up in an Army family, and graduated from high school in Northern Virginia. At West Point she played soccer, competed on the cross-country ski club, and sang in the Catholic Choir. At the beginning of her senior year, she was selected first captain — the highest ranking cadet in the Corps — the first woman to serve in that position. After graduation she became a Military Intelligence officer, serving in Bosnia at an intelligence system ground station, and in Europe as an anti-terrorism expert during the War on Terrorism. She served as strategic intelligence officer at U.S. Pacific Command, dealing with operations ranging from humanitarian assistance and disaster response to counterproliferation. She is married to another Army officer and has three children. She is now working in the intelligence field in Washington, D.C.

My father graduated from West Point in the class of 1966, and after my sophomore year in high school he took us back for a visit. We went to the West Point Museum, where I found myself captivated by the history of West Point as well as all that West Point graduates had accomplished. I surprised my family by deciding to apply. I later went to West Point on a candidate visit. Seeing the small classrooms, the low student to teacher ratio, and learning that the women's soccer team was going to become a Corps Squad, or varsity, sport my first year was all I needed to confirm that my decision had been a wise one.

Colonel Baker with her family in Hawaii.
Courtesy Kristin Baker

Shortly after learning I was accepted, my dad convinced me buy a pair of combat boots, soak them in the tub, and walk around the neighborhood to break them in. I felt like I stuck out like a sore thumb walking around the neighborhood as a high school senior in civilian clothes and combat boots, but I never got blisters from my boots when I arrived at West Point months later!

Most people assume that military kids have an advantage, but what I really had was a pair of broken-in boots and some basic knowledge that the Army consisted of officers and enlisted. My dad gave me advice, but I didn't have context yet to really understand what he was trying to tell me. People will tell you a thousand stories about their experiences at West Point, but it's difficult to understand them until you get there. Looking back on it after all these years, I suspect my dad was anxious about how I would react to my experiences as a new cadet.

I didn't know what to expect when I started Cadet Basic Training (CBT). I remember that I left my family at the stadium and got on a bus with a couple of dozen other new cadets, all bound for the tall gray buildings that would be our home for the next four years. Everybody looked tense and scared. I made a couple of jokes to try to lighten the mood, but no one even looked at me. It was a long, strange day until I arrived in my room and saw two other pairs of soccer cleats already tucked under the bunks. Both my roommates, it turned out, were also on the soccer team. I knew there would be an instant bond.

I enjoyed the military training aspect of CBT: learning to low crawl, fire a weapon, combatives training. I grew up as an athlete, which really helps. The mental challenge is the memorization — learning the front page and the sports page of the paper, memorizing dozens of cadet trivia, such as "How's the Cow?" all under pressure. The cow is full of lacteal fluid, or milk, for the record. And "How is she?" you might ask. She is as full of milk as there are servings of milk in the milk pitcher on your table at a meal. It sounds complicated, but you find little tricks to help you. If you enjoy challenges, you'll be fine.

It was a little overwhelming at the end of CBT when all the other cadets came back. There are all these new people to get to know — their personalities, likes and dislikes. I enjoyed the academic environment, where the challenges are intellectual, and success is all about intense time management on top of memorizing the sports page or the meal menu, shining your shoes, and cleaning your room to perfection!

Juggling sports, classes, and the daily rigors of cadet life can be difficult. I remember going on a trip [for soccer] and missing a key lesson, feeling daunted, thinking I was never going to catch up. The West Point instructors are incredible and they have such a fantastic Additional Instruction program. When you feel like you need help, both the civilian and military instructors will bend over backwards to help a struggling student.

After my third class year, I had the chance to be a drill cadet at Fort Jackson, South Carolina. I had to lead PT, teach military customs and courtesies, run ranges, and handle real crises just like the drill sergeants did. I couldn't help but think about how incredible the experience was. It also gave me better insight into what it's like to be enlisted. The next summer, I did an internship as a speechwriter for the Chief of Staff of the Army [at the Pentagon], and learned how policy is made at the top.

Being first captain was an interesting experience. Right after my selection was announced, I was surrounded by media. I went to all the morning talk shows. One of the supermarket tabloids even asked my mom for family photos. My cadet staff was fantastic, helping with all aspects of running the Corps of Cadets. They couldn't help me in dealing with the media nor all the speaking requests. Those seemed to come in like waves; one right after the other. The experience taught me how to be comfortable speaking in public, how to handle the media. I learned to accept that no [reporter] is every going to quote you quite right, but the vast majority of the media want to capture the story as accurately as possible.

To this day, whenever I'm in a leadership position, I find myself looking back on my experiences as a cadet. As an officer, you have to know how to make decisions quickly under extreme pressure. That's not difficult to do after you go through the new cadet/plebe experience. You learn how to absorb information quickly, sort through it, make decisions and stand by them.

You also gain a sense of responsibility that comes from the "No excuse" response you give as a plebe. When you make a mistake, it's your mistake. No blame, no excuses. You learn to step up and accept that it's your own fault and you'll fix it.

You also gain a certain level of confidence from having been in leadership positions. I have used that on every staff job. You have to know how to use your influence to get things done, even if you're not in charge and have very little authority.

I'll pass on some advice my dad gave me. He told me to remember that there's a lot of gamesmanship involved in your first year at West Point. The upperclass are pushing you, testing you, molding you. Their objective is to make you a better and stronger leader, capable of handling pressure, capable of excelling in what can often seem like a chaotic environment. I carried that advice with me throughout my first year. It helped me keep things in perspective.

I was lucky to have an incredibly supportive family. Finding that support while you are a cadet is important. For some it is family. For many it is their fellow cadets. For most it is a combination of the two.

Looking back, I can't imagine doing anything else as a career. I enjoy being part of something larger than any one individual, serving my nation, changing jobs, moving all the time, taking on new challenges. I have never once regretted going to West Point. It was the right choice for me.

Doctor (Lieutenant Colonel) Jessica Bunin, Class of 1996

Doctor Bunin graduated from high school in New Jersey, and was a varsity swimmer at West Point. She majored in chemistry and attended Tulane Medical School immediately after graduating. She completed her residency in psychiatry and internal medicine at Walter Reed followed by a critical care medicine fellowship. She completed a tour in Baghdad, Iraq, where her duties included taking care of soldiers who had just lost friends in combat, caring for soldiers dealing with the stresses of war, and detainee healthcare. She also completed a tour in Helmand Province, Afghanistan as a Critical Care Physician taking care of wounded US, British, Georgian and Afghani soldiers. She currently serves as Chief of Critical Care and Associate Program Director of the Internal Medicine Residency Program at Tripler Army Medical Center in Honolulu, Hawaii. She was recently inducted into the Order of Military Medical Merit. She is married to Special Agent Alexis Albano who is also a 1996 West Point graduate, and they live in Kaneohe, HI.

The New Jersey state swimming championships were always held at West Point, so I swam there every year from the time I was 10. By the time I was 12, I knew I wanted to go there, although I didn't really have a good idea of what that meant. I was recruited as a swimmer and got an appointment, but the week before I was supposed to report for R-Day, I had to have back surgery. So I spent the summer applying to other schools, and went to Brown for a year with every intention of returning to West Point the next academic year.

I had no military experience in my family, and CBT was a shock. I remember how hot it was, and how lost I felt. Every day, you never know what to expect. But I made good strong relationships in my squad, and I was involved with the Jewish Chapel, which was a nice safe haven.

When the academic year started, it was kind of a relief. It's hard for a woman competing physically all summer with men. The academics came naturally to me, and I had swimming to look forward to every day. Going to Brown for a year was beneficial in many ways. I took chemistry there, so I had a very good understanding of chemistry, which is really hard for some plebes. Also, some cadets crave the social experience of a civilian college, and I'd had a chance to get that out of my system.

I can't imagine having made it through the Academy without swimming. As a plebe, even when I felt I wasn't good at anything, I was good at that. The swim team gave me the chance

Bunin on deployment in Kuwait.
Courtesy Jessica Bunin

to see the upperclassmen as humans, a chance to get away from West Point and have some fun. Also, my parents came to a lot of swim meets, so I got to see them fairly often. All the doctors at West Point argue about that — the former varsity athletes can't imagine making it if they weren't athletes, and the non-athletes can't imagine surviving if they were!

Right after graduation, I went to medical school at Tulane. Academically, I don't know that West Point prepared me any better than my classmates. But I know that I never felt overwhelmed, because I'd balanced more than that as a cadet. I got cancer during my fourth year, but I managed to squeeze in all my classes and graduate on time. Then during my residency at Walter Reed, I got Hodgkin's disease, so with all the treatment my residency lasted six years. My next assignment was back at West Point.

Above all, West Point teaches you to work with people. You're in a leadership role 24/7, which forces you to learn a lot about how to work with people and how to deal with problems and crises. Leadership in a sorority is not the same — you can learn it other places in the Army, but not in the civilian world.

The bonds you make there last for life. There are graduates who see each other throughout their careers, because they're in the same branch. But for me, I disappeared for a number of years at medical school and doing my residency. Then when I was back at West Point, I was reintroduced to people I hadn't seen in a while. And the bonds are still there. It makes a difference, having gone through so much together. It creates a network that doesn't exist a lot of other places.

My advice to future cadets is to realize that there are so many aspects at West Point, you can't be good at everything. You're probably used to being the best at everything you're doing now, and it's hard to adjust to. You will experience failure. But you're going to get better at your weak areas, whether it's marksmanship, road marches, academics, or whatever. Just take it one day at a time and do your best.

When you have a problem getting along with other people, or someone is bothering you somehow, make an effort to resolve it diplomatically. Problems won't just go away on their own. They just get worse. That's an important lesson for later…it's conflict resolution on a smaller scale.

Have a thick skin. Growing up, I was the kind of kid who used to cry at everything. I learned not to be that way. Regardless of how harshly someone criticizes you, just take what you can from it to improve yourself, and let the rest roll right off your back.

Like medical school, looking back on my time at the Academy, I don't think I could do it again. But I don't think I would be a doctor if I had stayed at Brown. I needed that structure and discipline. West Point gave me the skills I needed to get through medical school. It was the best thing that could have happened to me.

Captain Walter Bryan Jackson, Class of 2005

Bryan Jackson was raised in a Navy family and attended three different high schools, graduating in Oak Harbor, Washington. After graduating from West Point, he was commissioned a field artillery officer and deployed to Iraq in 2006. Eight months into his tour and on patrol, his unit came under heavy machine gun fire. As he returned fire and helped a severely wounded soldier, he was shot in the thigh. He was hit again as he carried his wounded comrade to safety, refusing medical help until the other soldier could be treated. For his bravery, Captain Jackson was awarded the Distinguished Service Cross, the military's second highest award for valor, just below the Medal of Honor. After undergoing numerous surgeries and a lengthy rehab, he remained on active duty and served near the DMZ in Korea and later at Fort Sill, Oklahoma before being honorably discharged in 2011. He worked several years in oil & gas project management and in 2016 transitioned to the pharmacy industry where he currently works as a software product manager.

Growing up in a Navy family, my first thought was to go to Annapolis, but my SAT scores weren't quite high enough. The Navy Blue and Gold Officer really believed in me, and got me in touch with the West Point Field Force Officer, who helped me secure a nomination. I received the principal nomination from my Congressman, so I was pretty much guaranteed an appointment.[2]

I was also offered a four-year Marine ROTC scholarship, so I had that alternative. But what appealed to me about the Military Academy was the four years of total immersion in the military. I knew the regimented schedule would challenge me, and I would grow because of it. I didn't think I would get up at six a.m. for PT [physical training], or be that disciplined, if someone wasn't making me do it. So in that sense I knew it would be good for me. I wasn't in the best shape when I showed up for Beast Barracks. It was a lot more physically demanding than I thought it would be. But I enjoyed it for the most part — especially the camaraderie, meeting

Bryan Jackson is now a software product manager for a pharmacy company.
Courtesy Bryan Jackson

---

[2] For more information on the nomination process, see chapter 10.

strangers from all over the country, and also internationally, and learning to work as a team. I liked the different training challenges: rappelling, shooting, road marches, the obstacle course, getting toride in a Blackhawk helicopter. It was pretty intense — a crash course in Army life.

Plebe started, the 4:1 ratio of new cadets to year we were required to greet every upperclassmen or military officer we passed and would often be asked to recite knowledge to test our ability to think under pressure. The attack on 9-11 occurred about two months after I entered the Academy, and it really put into perspective why we were there.

The Academy is a cumulative, four-year process, and I took away both good and bad lessons from it. I put them into my leadership tool bag, and made sure I wouldn't repeat those mistakes later in life.

The Academy prepared me for deploying to Iraq and going into combat even better than the Army did, most of all by teaching me how to think and not what to think (an enduring theme at USMA). It also taught me about Servant Leadership. I learned that others are more likely to follow you when they realize you aren't there for yourself.

My advice if you're considering West Point is not to go for financial reasons or because your parents want you to go — something I remembered reading in a previous edition of this book. You should go because you want to go, for your own reasons and your own growth.

Mental preparation is really important. Make sure your head is in the right place, that you know what you're getting into. Know that the Academy will be a challenge. It's the same mental preparation you go through before you go into combat. You have to get yourself mentally ready. At times you will doubt why you chose this path, and that's totally normal to feel that way. Don't give up or take yourself too seriously; take everything that happens with a grain of salt. Learn from your mistakes, and try not to repeat them. When things get tough, fall back on your faith, family and friends. Remember that a positive mental attitude can get you through anything.

Captain Shaye Haver, Class of 2012

Raised in an Army family, Captain Haver graduated from high school in Texas before entering West Point. Following graduation, she attended flight school at Fort Rucker, Georgia. In 2015, she became one of the first women to graduate from Ranger School. She is currently at Fort Benning, Georgia.

When I was in high school, my dad got stationed at Ford Hood, Texas, and we lived in Copperas Cove. It was the first time I had been in a public school, and I was trying to fit in, so I joined Army JROTC. I was really inspired by the cadre, and I decided to apply to West Point. I also found Army life appealing—the idea of service, flying like my dad did, and having a way to pay for college.

After I was accepted, I went for a visit. It was April, and the campus totally sucked me in. I knew right away that I belonged there. It was gorgeous, and the history is just thriving everywhere.

I had no idea what to expect in CBT. I had asked some grads about it, but they all just said you won't know until you experience it yourself. You get about 30 seconds to say goodbye to your family; it happens very fast. But I realized very quickly, at the end of that 30 seconds, that I was on my own. I was used to discipline, and it wasn't hard to adjust. The one thing that was a bit strange was getting used to being yelled at by someone just two years older. I really loved CBT, seeing myself transform from a puny high school kid into a soldier, and it was all due to the cadre and everything they taught me. I loved being out in the field, getting introduced to new things such as weapons and the branches of the military.

Captain Haver visits West Point with fellow Ranger, Captain Kristen Geist. *United States Military Academy*

Our class scrambled after CBT, so that meant we had to get to know new people and new leadership styles. The academic schedule is heavy, plus you have duties as a member of a company, and you have to keep your room and uniforms up. Academics were challenging, but I was ready for the challenge. It forced me to learn time management in a big way. I knew right away that, if I was going to good grades, I was going to be responsible for it, find tutoring when I needed it, etc.

I had hoped to play soccer at West Point, but I ended up not playing, which gave me the chance to do club sports. I did triathlon, which gave me a passion for endurance sports. I did rock climbing, so I got outdoors, off campus, and had a chance to experience and appreciate the northeastern United States. I was also was on the strength and conditioning team. For company intramurals, I did Sandhurst to help out my company and develop esprit de corps. [Sandhurst is a competition that pits 9-member squads against each other, performing a series of military tasks that are both physically and mentally challenging.]

Sandhurst helped drive me to be in leadership positions. I was a platoon leader and company physical development officer. As the physical development officer, I helped people who were struggling to meet the physical fitness standards. My classmates joked that I kicked people out of West Point. I was really there to help, but if they didn't want to do the work, they would get kicked out.

I spent 18 months at Fort Rucker doing flight training, dunker training, survival school, and the Basic Army Officer Course. Time management was the most important thing I learned at West Point that helped me at Fort Rucker. I was also comfortable with the knowledge requirements, making timely decisions, being able to respond quickly to any demand. Flight school is study-intensive—you might have classes in systems, weather, and physics all on the same day, and I did well academically because I was used to working in a fast-paced environment.

I went to Ranger School because I wanted to gain a better understanding of how ground forces operate, so I can keep them alive. When I got there, I saw the importance of peer leadership. You don't wear your Army rank there. You have to be creative, learn from others, and be decisive. I think West Point is a four-year course in how to be a platoon leader, plus I'd been doing that for 24 months since graduation. I understood the weight of that. You learn how to build a team; the importance of the team in succeeding at a no-fail mission.

At first my Ranger classmates were just curious about the women going through, but then they saw that we were required to meet the same standards and do all the same tasks, so they accepted us as part of the team. We all adjusted as we went through.
On Veterans Day, I went to the Vice President's house, and sat with Michelle Obama and talked with her. The response from my fellow soldiers has been very positive overall, though I'm tired of taking selfies!

My advice to candidates is to be well rounded. You will be required to be a soldier, a scholar, and an athlete. So volunteer, play sports. When you get to West Point, embrace every opportunity. The academics are no joke, so you have to be responsible for your own success. Don't take the summer training for granted, because you will learn valuable soldier skills. Once you graduate, you're on the job. Moms and dads will be putting their children's lives in your hands. Remember it's a great privilege to lead America's sons and daughters.

HOW TO PREPARE

CHAPTER 4

Mental Preparation Must Come First

Throughout this book you will hear cadets and graduates talk about the challenges of the Academy — the stress, long hours, and lack of sleep that come with the difficult academic load, the physical demands, and the exacting military training. Yet the "Long Gray Line" of West Point graduates continues to get longer. Just how do so many cadets survive all four years and graduate?

When you talk to Academy graduates (and we strongly encourage you to do just that), nearly all of them will tell you that mental preparation is the most important factor to making it through. If your mind is properly prepared, all of the stress and all of the challenges will be easier for you to endure. If not, then you will wake up each day questioning why you are there. You will meet each challenge thinking about your family back home or your friends at State U. If you do not have the right mindset, you will be miserable, and you will most likely come face to face with something new: failure.

Those who fail are usually those who have not mentally prepared themselves.

GOALS: THE RIGHT MOTIVATION TO SUCCEED

Those who lose sight of their goals, or who never had the right ones in the first place, are usually the first to fall. To survive, you MUST have unwavering goals. You MUST have reasons, good reasons, not to give up. If you do not wake up each day knowing why you are enduring the rigors of Academy life, every day will seem endless and pointless.

The reasons young men and women choose West Point are individual and complex. But after conducting hundreds of interviews, some common motives began to appear again and again. We will examine each of them and see if any of them might motivate you, or create problems for you.

I WANT A FREE, QUALITY EDUCATION. This is a good reason to go to the Academy. West Point is considered an outstanding academic institution with superb professors, receiving top ratings in nation-wide surveys. Those who want a great education are seldom disappointed. But even the most enthusiastic scholars have to divide their attention between academic, military, and physical demands. So if you want to focus solely on your education, a traditional college may be a better choice. Also, if you want to be highly specialized in one field of study, you may find the Academy's large and diverse core curriculum is not for you. The Academy education is designed to prepare well-rounded leaders for military service.

Most cadets laugh when someone says their education is "free." Their parents might see it that way, but they have to earn that education every single day, with hard work and complete dedication of body and mind. Also, you will have to "pay back" that "free" education.

If you graduate, you are obligated to serve on active duty in the Army for five years. Furthermore, you should also realize that these required terms of duty can change at any time, even while you are in the Academy.

Nine years — four years at the Academy and five as an officer — may seem like an enormous amount of time when you are only 17 years old. Of course, you will be compensated with money and benefits during all those years, and the pay could be about what you would make after graduating from a civilian college. You will also see the world and gain experiences you cannot find elsewhere — especially leadership experience that later becomes highly attractive to corporate recruiters. But you will be expected to perform whatever job you are assigned to the best of your ability, and live wherever the Army assigns you. You cannot just quit as you might in a civilian job.

I WANT A CHALLENGE. Some cadets are attracted to the Academy precisely because they know it will be a challenge. Some like the discipline and military training. Others want a tough and well-respected academic experience. These are smart, competitive people who never felt pushed or challenged in high school. They want to take on something difficult to prove to themselves they can do it, learn their strengths and limitations, and make themselves better.

For those who come deliberately seeking a challenge, few are disappointed. Most cadets say that no single aspect of the Academy — academics, military training, or physical demands — is very difficult. But taken together, those demands tax every ounce of your capability. And if the basic requirements are not challenging enough, they can take on a double major, become leaders within the Corps of Cadets, or get involved in extra-curricular

For those who want to be pushed to the limit, West Point is a great opportunity. *United States Military Academy*

activities. Surrounded by other equally capable, equally competitive young men and women, they often find they push one other to work even harder. The Academy is an ideal place for those who want to find their own limits and be pushed to do their best.

I WANT TO PLAY DIVISION I SPORTS. The Academy may offer an opportunity to play NCAA Division I varsity sports that a student would not have at a civilian college. West

Point must recruit candidates who are not only competitive athletes, but who also have strong academic records, demonstrated leadership ability, and a commitment to serve their country. Ohio State and UCLA have a much broader pool from which to recruit.

Athletes must understand (or learn quickly) that regardless how dedicate they are as athletes, the Academy's mission is to turn them into Army officers. After graduating, their chances to play professional sports are nearly nonexistent, and practicing their sport must fit into a schedule jammed with academic and military responsibilities. However, for athletes who want to play in a superb program while getting an outstanding education and a guaranteed job, West Point is a good place to be. Most cadet athletes we talked to said they came to West Point to become an Army officer, and their sport was just an added benefit that made their four years as a cadet more enjoyable.

MY FATHER/MOTHER/GRANDPARENTS WANT ME TO GO. Whether we are talking to parents, cadets, or graduates, the most common request we hear goes something like this: Make sure you tell candidates to make sure they are coming because THEY want to, not their relatives. We heard countless sad stories about cadets who found themselves at the Academy living out someone else's dream. This is definitely a bad reason to go to the Academy.

Perhaps they had a parent or grandparent who graduated from the Academy who is eager to see the family tradition go on. Perhaps their mother or father sees the Academy as a way out of paying college tuition, or an opportunity so good that no one should pass it up.

Nearly every group of cadets, when asked about their classmates who quit, cited an example of someone who came because mom or dad wanted them to. These situations almost never have happy endings. Most agreed that you can tough it out if you are there for yourself, but it is too hard to do for someone else. There are occasionally sad tales, such as one that involved a young woman from a difficult home environment. Her mother told her that if she quit, she was on her own. The cadet's belongings and a small check arrived by mail at West Point, the mother's only small act of support.

Military Academy Liaison Officers (MALOs interview all candidates on behalf of the Academy) and congressional nomination panels are constantly on the lookout for overenthusiastic parents of underenthusiastic candidates. They usually offer an opportunity for the candidate to bow out — such a candidate will not be offered an appointment and the parents will never know why. Said one MALO, "There's no point in applying if someone pushed them into it. I can tell early on in the conversation where they're coming from. If they aren't personally motivated, they won't make it through."

I WANT TO GO FOR THE GLAMOUR AND RECOGNITION. This is a bad reason, but who would admit to it? Nobody, probably. But young people can get caught up in their egos without ever realizing that it's happening. A typical example is the student who says to a teacher or counselor at school, "Oh, I'm thinking about West Point as a possible college."

Everyone gets excited…the counselor, the parents, the teachers. Soon word is out that this superstar is headed for West Point — after all, the student is sure to be accepted.

One thing leads to another and the student gets swept up in the process — and all the new attention feeds the ego. Letters start arriving from the Academy. Then there is the contact with a congressman or senator and a follow-up letter. Heady stuff to be sure.

Now the pressure is mounting. Something that seemed like a good idea just to explore is now a steamroller picking up momentum. And the student may begin having doubts, but does not want to disappoint those who are now working hard to help him.

Next come the medical examination, the physical fitness test and the interviews. Facing those challenges the student says, "Hey, I'm can do this. I'm up for the challenge. I'm going to show these people that I've got the right stuff."

And he makes it. Suddenly he really is a hero because he is ACCEPTED! All he has to do is read the local newspaper where his honor is announced, or watch the audience at graduation as they applaud his magnificent achievement. Neighbors and relatives call to say how proud they are.

Being appointed to West Point does make you special, but don't expect to be treated that way!
United States Military Academy

Then what? CBT and the non-stop stress. The academic year starts and he is starved for sleep and struggling to pass his classes for the first time in his life. He is constantly being criticized and corrected. This is the glamorous life he had envisioned?

Nobody wants to admit that he or she is at the Academy for glamour and recognition. They end up embarrassed and demoralized…and they usually quit.

I WANT TO BE AN ARMY OFFICER. This is the best reason of all, IF you know WHY you want to be an officer. The complete four-year Academy program is valued at around $350,000. Those taxpayer dollars are intended to be an investment in a career officer.

Try answering the following questions. If you say "yes" to most of them, you are mentally prepared with the best reasons for going to the Academy.

▶ Do you want to serve your country and defend its freedoms? Are you prepared to go wherever the nation needs you, even into combat?

▶ Do you enjoy the challenges of leadership?

▶ Do you want heavy responsibility at a much younger age than you could expect in a civilian job?

▶ Do you want to become a better person?
▶ Do you respect military tradition?
▶ Do you want to be an officer so you can lead solders in combat?
▶ Do you look forward to the challenge of a new assignment every three or four years instead of just one lifelong job?
▶ Do you want more job security than you would have in most civilian jobs?
▶ Do you want to be able to retire at an age young enough to start another career?

In summary, there are GOOD REASONS and BAD REASONS for going to the Academy. The first step in getting your mind prepared for the Academy is to know that you are going for the GOOD REASONS.

If you are going for the BAD REASONS, consider doing yourself a favor by stopping right now, even if it means disappointing your parents or grandparents. If you do not, you can expect to have an unhappy, and perhaps short, career as a cadet — which would eventually lead to even greater disappointment for your relatives, and many regrets for you.

KNOW WHAT TO EXPECT

The second thing you should do in preparing your mind for the Academy is to know what to expect when you get there.

In combat and in training, an Army lieutenant will receive an operation order from his or her captain. The first thing always covered is the "situation" — knowing details about the enemy forces, who and where the friendly forces will be, and what the environment is like when it comes to weather, terrain, and other challenges.

When you get ready to take on four years at the Academy, you must also understand what kind of environment and challenges you will be facing. Reading this book is a good first step. But there are several other things that are recommended.

Get in touch with your MALO. Every high school in the nation has a West Point representative (details in Chapter 9). If you let him or her know you are interested in West Point, they can connect you with opportunities to meet cadets home on vacation and graduates who live in your area, or let you know about service academy information days or other events.

Search for other Army officers who will talk with you. They are almost always eager to advise students, especially the retired officers who have extra time. Tell them you are thinking about applying to the Academy and you are wondering what being an officer is really like. At the interview ask the hard questions, such as, What happens when an officer does not get promoted? If officers make a mistake, what happens to them? How does it feel to come under fire in combat?

The BEST thing for you to do is VISIT THE ACADEMY. When you get there, see what Academy life is like, talk to cadets and staff, and try to picture yourself there. You can compete to attend the week-long Summer Leaders Experience (go to the admissions website and click on Summer Program), attend a sports camp (see **goarmywestpoint.com/**

camps) or arrange a visit with the Admissions Office. These programs are discussed in more detail in Chapter 8.

The cadets who visited the Academy before going there all said that it helped them because they knew what to expect. A visit also shows your MALO and congressional interview panel that you are committed and enthusiastic enough about attending the Academy that you are willing to do some "homework" on your own.

Some candidates decide NOT to apply after a visit, but that is fine — West Point and you are better off if you learn that the Academy is not for you before you accept an appointment.

DETERMINATION

Mental preparation for the Academy must include one more task. That task is to convince yourself that you are going to succeed when you get there. You cannot be a quitter.

Thousands and thousands of graduates before you have made it through. If you made it through the competitive admissions process, you DO have what it takes to succeed, if you are willing to work hard, and if you are determined.

Tips in this book and advice from your classmates will help you get through the hard times. But only if you resolve to make it through before you start CBT.

If you do realize that the Academy is really not the right place for you, we recommend you resolve to make it through your plebe year before you leave. By sticking it out for a full year, you will benefit several ways:

First, you will come away with college credits you can transfer to just about any school in the nation. You will also have learned more about yourself than you would as a freshman at another college.

If you stay through the first year, you will never doubt whether you could have made it. You can be assured that you are leaving on your own terms.

At the end of the year, something else might happen: you might change your mind. You might realize the worst is behind you and the rest is not so bad after all. You might become so close to your classmates that you want to stay with them and serve alongside them. You might realize that West Point and the Army are exactly where you belong.

A final note: Many cadets and graduates will tell you they thought about quitting, either seriously or in response to a bad day. They will tell you they talked to another cadet, an officer or other mentor, or their parents about what they were feeling. Then they decided to stay after all, and were very glad they did. But those who quit usually have tremendous lifelong regrets.

CHAPTER 5

Expect to Experience Academic Shock

After breezing through high school with minimal effort, being told how smart they are, most cadets are quickly humbled when they start taking academic classes at the U.S. Military Academy. They are shocked to find themselves struggling as they never have before.

What's the problem? Why should cadets who have scored high on ACT and SAT tests, and graduated near the top of their high school classes, encounter so much trouble with course work at the Academy?

There are at least six reasons, many of which can be traced back to habits formed in high school.

★ PROBLEM ONE: Competition

In Chapter 3, you read the stories of some graduates who struggled academically. Their stories are not unique. Most of the cadets who come to the Academy have been the top students in their high schools. Recent classes have entered with average SAT scores over 600 in verbal, writing, and math; more than two thirds of the last entering class were National Honor Society members. Most are competitive by nature, taking hard classes and getting the best grades, ensuring they are at the top of their class.

But how much competition did they really have? Most took classes with students with all ranges of abilities and motivation. Many cadets said that they were able to get good grades in high school without much effort. Several admitted that they just listened in class and relied on their natural learning ability. They relied on the teacher to make sure they understood the material, not on themselves.

Now try to imagine what happens when all of these "good" students get into classes together at the Academy. Suddenly the competitive situation is drastically different. The competition is now fierce, and a large number of former "good" students end up on the bottom half of the grade curve. Students who were use to seeing easy grades of "A" are suddenly looking at "C's" or worse.

As one cadet explained, "Most people had it easy in high school and just breezed through their senior year. I had to learn how to study. It took all of my fourthclass year…[to learn] notetaking and studying in general."

★ PROBLEM TWO: Overload

Most high school students, even the overachievers who receive appointments to service academies, do not experience much stress getting their school work done. Even with extracurricular activities, sports, or a part-time job, finding enough hours to do all you need to has not been a real challenge. At the Academy, that will change.

Besides taking 18-21 semester hours of challenging courses (compared to perhaps 15 hours their civilian counterparts must take), a cadet has mandatory athletic and military training every day. During the plebe year, many cadets will discover that the techniques that worked in high school do not work at West Point. According to a former vice dean, there are always some cadets who will be "surprised by the academic rigor and the amount of time required to be successful." In fact, nearly every cadet and graduate interviewed mentioned time management as the biggest challenge at West Point.

They may procrastinate, as they did in high school, until the night before a big assignment or paper is due. Then they realize they have other things that have to get done, or the assignment takes longer than they expected. The result is a poorly done assignment completed at 2 a.m., and a cadet who cannot stay awake in class the next day.

Or they resolve to do every assignment for the next day to the best of their ability, read every word on every page, and even spend extra time on material that is giving them trouble. Using that approach in high school meant they got top grades in their classes. But by midnight their brain is begging for sleep, and they still have two of their four assignments left to do.

Many cadets and graduates talked about the importance — and challenge — of balancing academics and the many other demands on their time. Succeeding academically means figuring out how to strike that balance. Throughout this book, you will read advice about how to do that.

★ PROBLEM THREE: Letter Hunters

If you are now a student, look around during one of your classes, then ask yourself this question: What do these students, myself included, really want out of this class? If you are objective, you will probably come up with this answer: "A's" or maybe "B's."

Are you a letter hunter? Or are you really trying to learn the material? In chemistry class do you really want to understand the significance of Avogadro's Number? In history class do you really want to know how the Missouri Compromise affected the next one hundred years of life in America? In advanced algebra class do you really want to know how quadratic equations can help you solve a whole new class of problems?

Or are you memorizing all those things just long enough to get the letters that you want? Many "good" students are letter hunters. They do whatever is necessary to get the first letter or two in the alphabet. Then they go on to the next letter-hunting challenge. They are often more concerned about pleasing the teacher who assigns the grade than they are about learning the material being taught. As a result, sometimes they do not learn much at all.

So what awaits a "good" student when professors at the Academy expect a cadet to have high school-level knowledge of algebra or history or chemistry? In fact, algebra is often cited by professors as a weak area — many high school students get past algebra with A's early in their career, and move on to trigonometry and calculus without really having a thorough knowledge of algebra and how to apply it.

Just having good grades from high school will not cut it. The professors at the Academy are not interested in your high school grades. They ARE interested in building on knowledge that you were supposed to have gained during your high school years.

So be warned. Those who go to West Point with just a good GPA, rather than knowledge, had better expect some hard times.

★ PROBLEM FOUR: Escape Artists

Many "good" high school students have a bag of tricks they can use to escape detection when they come to class unprepared. Some look at their desks and remain silent if the teacher asks for volunteers to answer questions. This works especially well in large classes. It is easy to vanish in the crowd.

Another trick is leave the textbook open and scan the lesson rapidly before the teacher begins asking questions. This is a favorite of those who are good readers.

One of the best tricks, when the teacher is not alert, is to listen carefully to what the teacher has said and then volunteer when one of the questions has an obvious answer. That gets the student off the hook, usually for the whole class period. After dodging one bullet, a student is not likely to get shot at again, especially in a big class.

If you happen to be a "good" student, you can probably add your own favorite techniques to this list. Students have probably been creating them forever. But realize that you might as well leave your bag of tricks at home if you go to the Academy.

Why? Because the classes are small — usually 18 or less — and every professor will know your name and something about you within a day or two after you start a class. Moreover, your professors believe strongly in ACCOUNTABILITY.

This means that they will hold you responsible for whatever reading or homework they assigned. More important, unlike your high school teachers who were burdened with large student loads, they will do some kind of accounting that will let them know how well you did your assignment, in accordance with the Thayer philosophy of instruction.

That might be a quiz or a homework check. It might be a barrage of questions that you cannot escape. Very often, it will be a trip to the front of the class or to the board so your knowledge, or lack of it, can be displayed for the whole class. Very often they will move through the material so quickly that, if you are "faking it," you will soon find yourself totally lost.

Escape artists do not do well at the Academy. In small classes with determined professors there is no way to dodge the bullets. And if you try, you are sure to get wounded.

★ PROBLEM FIVE: Copiers

Some "good" students are able to get the grades they want in high school by cheating. But they present little problem at the Academy because cadets with that kind of character rarely survive.

The "copiers" who do have problems at the Academy are not necessarily cheaters, at least not intentionally. On the contrary, they are often very conscientious students.

Are you a "copier?" Here is how to tell. What do you do if your teacher gives a reading assignment and also asks that you write out the answers to certain questions that are at the end of the chapter?

Do you read the assignment two or three times, or whatever it takes to understand it thoroughly? Then do you write out the answers to the questions in your own words, thinking as you write, and taking pride in your good grammar, punctuation and spelling? And finally, do you proofread your answers to make sure you gave the best possible answer, free of errors?

If so, pat yourself on the back and consider yourself unique. You will probably do well at West Point.

Or do you answer the questions by simply copying the relevant sentence or two from the assigned chapter? Do you finish the homework without even thinking about what you just wrote, or how it relates to other lessons in the same class?

Some high school teachers even encourage this kind of copying. It is much easier to grade the homework or a test if they see the familiar words right out of the textbook.

How do you go about writing a paper? Do you cut and paste whole sentences and even paragraphs word-for-word right off of a web site? Of course, the serious letter hunters will not stop at that. They also will copy something from an additional web site or maybe even a library book, "just to be safe."

The problem with copiers is that they have not learned how to organize their thoughts, synthesize multiple ideas into new ideas, and write them in a logical, systematic manner. This is a serious handicap at the Academy, because there is a heavy emphasis on developing just that skill.

A very important part of an officer's job is writing reports. So writing is required in most classes — not just in English classes — and a student who has been a copier is in immediate trouble with such assignments. Cadets are expected to synthesize and understand what they have read, not just copy it. Even more seriously, if a copier at the Academy fails to acknowledge his or her sources, it may constitute cheating, an Honor Concept violation which can result in dismissal.

Writing cannot be learned without practice. The copier has to get that practice at the worst possible time — when all the other pressures on the plebes are at their maximum.

★ PROBLEM SIX: Senioritis

Teachers who love teaching, who would never want to do anything else, who think it is the greatest job in the world, seldom like teaching seniors during their final semester in high school.

The reason: senioritis, a behavior pattern where seniors coast through the last weeks of school with the least effort possible.

Many excuses are used to justify such behavior. "I'm burned out on school." "I have worked long enough; now I want to play." "I just can't get going any more." "I already got accepted to the college I want to go to."   Have you heard any of those excuses? You will if you are not yet a senior. But just remember, if you are planning on going to the Academy, senioritis is a serious affliction.

It is during the senior year that high school students have the opportunity to take the kinds of classes that will help them the most at the Academy. This is the year when high-level math, science or English courses can be taken. This is the year when creative writing is most likely to be an elective. This is the year when Advanced Placement college courses are available. Most important, this is the time when one's learning curve and study habits should be PEAKING, not declining.

Students who hit the Academy running and in peak form suffer less stress than those who are out of shape mentally or physically. If you are lazy your senior year in high school, beware. The Academy is likely to be harder on you than for those who managed to escape the problem.

★ PROBLEM SEVEN: Sit-and-Get Learning

Sit-and-get learners are the product of a type of teaching common in high schools. Smart high school students, the kind of students who become candidates for a service academy, are often very successful with this kind of learning. And high school teachers are often their accomplices. The students sit in class like an empty cup into which the teacher pours knowledge until the cup is sufficiently full.

Consider the following classroom scenario: The teacher, Mr. Spoonfeeder, assigns a chapter in the science textbook on Monday. On Tuesday, he reviews all the material from that chapter that he feels is important — those things he will cover on the test. He will explain it in great detail, and because he is a conscientious teacher, he will then ask questions to make sure the students understand it.

The next day, he will hand out worksheets in class, watching as his students

You won't be allowed to sit back and listen passively; you will have to demonstrate what you have learned. *United States Military Academy*

complete all the questions. If anyone has a question, he is right there to explain the concept again and help the student get to the right answer.

On Thursday, he decides that the concepts were awfully difficult and most of the students are struggling. So he works hard to come up with another method of explaining the lesson, just to make sure everyone grasps it. On Friday, he reviews sample test questions in class, just to make absolutely sure the students are ready for the test.

Most cadets will come to the Academy having had teachers like this. They have been spoonfed for years by conscientious teachers who believed that they were doing what was best for their students. The smarter students know that if they do not grasp the material the first time it is presented, Mr. Spoonfeeder will surely explain it again. All they have to do is keep coming to class and paying attention, and Mr. Spoonfeeder will make sure they learn what they need to know. Unfortunately, those students never had the opportunity to learn HOW TO LEARN on their own.

And what do they find at the Academy?

Professor Independence. The faculty is loaded with them. Those professors give assignments and hold cadets accountable for knowing AND understanding the material the minute they arrive in class. They will move on quickly, and any cadet who does not grasp the concepts taught will have to ask for extra help OUTSIDE of class. If they do not, they will be left behind.

Why? Because they have to do it to train the kinds of officers needed by the Army.

Officers must be efficient, independent learners in order to keep on top of rapidly-evolving technology and operate in a dynamic world. As the vice dean explained, "It's difficult by design. It helps them grow into better leaders." The professors will expect you to develop the appetite and ability to learn — and understand — complex ideas. Lives will depend on you. That is why they teach the way they do.

So you should not be surprised by the difficulty of the academic load at the Academy. But how can you be prepared for those academic challenges?

A NEW ATTITUDE TOWARD LEARNING

If you still have a year or more left of your high school career, the best advice is to CHANGE YOUR ATTITUDE. Stop thinking of your homework and test preparation in terms of doing enough to get an A. Instead, try to get the most learning you can from every class and every task. Your classmates may think you are a little weird, but you are not going to the same college they are.

One approach is to change your attitude about competition. If there is little competition in your classes, pretend that you are in a class with students who are all as capable as yourself. Get in the habit of always doing more than you are assigned. Learn to take pride in giving 150 percent effort in the classroom.

You are probably an athlete of some kind. Bring your competitive attitude from the playing field into the classroom. Take pride in never letting up. Treat your course work like an opponent. Master it, not just

Academics at West Point require you to take responsibility for your own learning. *United States Military Academy*

halfway, but completely.

Also, you should change your attitude about what you want to get out of your classes. Despite what has been said about letter hunting, there is nothing wrong with getting good grades. In fact, you have to have a lot of the good ones just to be accepted at the Academy. But letter hunting should not be your MAIN goal. Your main goal should be learning the material in your courses.

If you will do that, and you do it well, and you really try to remember what you have learned, the good letters will come. You do not sacrifice anything by going after knowledge rather than letters. Instead, you get a two-fer: you get the knowledge AND the letters.

Are you an escape artist? If you are the type of person who continually wants to slide by without doing assigned work, your tricks might get you into the Academy, but you will not last. If you are that type of person, the upperclassmen and professors will find you out. They will make sure you do not survive long enough to create problems as an officer.

Do you even need to be told that you should quit copying your reports and answers to questions out of books? If you are going through the motions of completing a homework assignment without learning a thing, you are going about it the wrong way. So bite the bullet. Start writing material out of your head instead of out of a book. The effort might be painful at first. But it has never been known to cause brain damage. Your brain is like your muscles — it has to be in shape for you to succeed at West Point.

Will you catch senioritis? This is a problem you can avoid if you are determined. How? By deliberately taking the hardest courses you can during your senior year and developing a special attitude about those courses. Believe that they are more important than anything else you have taken in high school. Then go after them with determination.

Learn everything that there is to learn in those courses, and more. Once you have committed yourself to this kind of effort, you will not have time to catch senioritis. And when you get to the Academy, you will be up to speed and have one less problem to worry about.

What if you are a sit-and-get learner? Your main problem, if you are still in high school, is that you cannot control the methods that your teachers use. And you are not likely to find many Mr. Independences in your high school. But you are not helpless. Be as prepared as you can possibly be. Even make it a game to try to know more about the subject than the teacher knows, or keep track of everything the teacher says that you didn't already know.

HOW TO PREPARE ACADEMICALLY

Besides developing the proper attitude about learning, what else should you do to prepare for the Academy?

You should take all of the math courses that are available in your high school. Take four years of English and four years of a foreign language if that is possible. Take chemistry and physics — advanced courses if you can.

Take computer courses. All cadets are issued a laptop computer, and you will find that your computer is used to manage nearly every aspect of your life. You may have to e-mail a homework assignment to your instructor, use a computer-aided design program for an engineering project, or collaborate on line to complete a team project.

If you are not comfortable using most common computer programs, you will add to your workload and stress level. If you can take some programming classes, you will have an advantage in the challenging computer science class. A math professor advises that you "dig into [Microsoft] Excel. Get familiar with it, or another spreadsheet."

Many candidates for the Academy take Advanced Placement, or AP, classes. Most cadets and instructors will tell you those AP classes will help you validate core courses or have an easier time in the first semester or two. One word of caveat: Make sure you actually learn what the AP classes teach, and remember the material in the classes leading up to the AP class. AP Calculus is an example. You must come to the Academy with a good, working comprehension of the algebra and trigonometry you took in high school. And if you test out of Calculus 1 and go immediately to Calculus 2, you must retain, understand, and be able to apply all you were supposed to have learned. All the warnings at the beginning of this chapter apply.

Speech (or debate) is an excellent course if you have room in your schedule for an elective. The practice of speaking before a group builds confidence. And it gives you practice thinking on your feet. You will appreciate that experience if you go to the Academy because you will have to stand up and speak in front of your peers.

If you are a slow reader, a reading class that teaches speed, comprehension, and recall will be a great investment. Plowing through several hundred pages a night is not unusual. Being an efficient reader will help you get through all your assignments and still get a reasonable night's sleep.

A final bit of advice has to do with study techniques. Each night, before you start studying, look over all the assignments. Quickly turn through the pages of your textbooks and try to estimate how long it should take you to do each assignment. Then give yourself a time allotment for each one. Leave time, also, for breaks. Later, when you finish studying, give yourself a "grade" on how closely your study time matched your estimates.

Start pushing yourself. Try to shorten the study time by pretending that you have other things to do. Get in the habit of planning your entire week, looking ahead at upcoming papers, projects, tests, and quizzes. Schedule time for each one, and try to stick to the schedule.

This is realistic study practice, because at the Academy your assignments will be long and the time to do them will be limited. You will rarely have enough time to study as much as you would like. You will have to prioritize and make compromises. By learning to do that in high school, you will have one less thing to learn in the high-pressure environment of West Point.

A chemistry professor sums it up well: "Don't slack off your senior year. Put some effort into focusing of fundamental skills, and developing good study habits. You have to take ownership of your own learning."

CHAPTER 6

Professors' Advice About Academic Preparation

Many plebes struggle with academics, at least at first. The most common cause of problems has to do with time. As a cadet, you will be expected to prepare for two hours for every one hour of class time. Finding time in the day for all this preparation, let alone studying for tests, is difficult.

Time management is something to you must learn to deal with at West Point. But is there anything else you can do to be prepared for the academic challenges ahead? We talked to professors from a variety of subjects, including those who teach the classes that tend to trip up plebes, for their advice.

READING, WRITING...

You may think that being an Army officer is more about combat tactics and weapons than communications; but the ability to read, write, and speak well are essential skills for an officer. You must be able to construct clear, simple, grammatically correct sentences that communicate effectively. Lives may be on the line.

A current English professor who is the course director for the freshman English class says, "Read more. Reading good writing makes good writers. It helps you learn about style and technique. Read works that aren't assigned by your [high school] English teachers." He recommends you look online for anthologies of great books.

Another English professor offered similar advice: "I would just emphasize that they should read as much as possible and read critically, which means that they should think about what they read."

Even the chemistry department sees problems that are based in reading, rather than knowledge of chemistry. "Sometimes they come in with poor reading skills. They lack the ability to read and decipher the problems."

Another chemistry professor offered specific advice on how to read a textbook: "Go through a chapter the first time and highlight the important concepts — things to learn — and we have printed course objectives the student can follow, so there's never a question or any decision to make on what to study and what to bypass. Then I recommend they go back over the chapter, and I personally like to take notes. By writing things down, I remember them better. Some will say, 'Well, the high school text I used in Kansas was easy to read and I didn't have to do all of that.' My answer: "You're not in Kansas anymore.'"

Writing assignments are part of many subjects at any college, not just English. At West Point, you will be required to write up chemistry labs and research papers for history, or briefings for military studies classes. Will you be prepared?

Said an English professor, "Most cadets are capable of doing the work. The writing assignments are not too onerous, especially at first. The problem is time management." In other words, writing takes thought and time in order to be logical, organized, and focused. If you are in the habit of waiting until the last minute, your writing will not be as good.

Another English professor expressed the same concern: They wait until it's very late in the process to get started. Even though we've had two days of workshopping and they've had a chance to develop their text, they still haven't focused on the subject of their paper. Then at the last minute, they write a paper that's unfocused. It falls apart because it's just based upon ideas. They haven't worked carefully because they haven't thought carefully."

And yet another explained, "Writing is dependent on the situation. Be ready with the right mindset. You need to know how to write an argument — which means making a claim and supporting it with evidence. That's the mark of "discourse."

In high school, you may have been getting good grades by writing your papers at the last minute. Instead, get into the habit of writing them ahead of time, planning what you will say and organizing your thoughts. According to the freshman English professor, "Start early. You may have started papers the night before and got As in high school. That's not how good writing is done. That approach will get you a C- here."

You should make time to write a draft, revise, and revise again. If you can get comfortable with this process, you will turn in better assignments. If you can practice this approach to writing papers in high school, you will have an easier time at West Point.

You should also learn to do research, including understanding what constitutes a reliable source and how to take multiple references and form your own conclusion. "First thing, they have to have something to say, which means they have to read carefully. They have to be able to do more than summarize what they have read."

... AND ARITHMETIC

Math has two purposes at West Point, according to the head of the math department. "We're trying to prepare the cadets for engineering and physics. But we also teach math for its own sake, the quantitative reasoning leaders will need, and the ability to operate in a technology rich environment."

He goes on to explain, "A lot of cadets think they know what math is. They're surprised by what happens in college. We don't do routine calculations. Here, it's more about concepts and patterns."

Many professors commented on the importance — and for many cadets, lack — of solid algebra skills. Said a chemistry professor, "There's no calculus required in the core chemistry classes. But we see that algebra skills are generally poor. They make mistakes with simple common denominators. When you add one algebraic manipulation, we see a 10% drop in the number of right answers."

Another math professor emphasized being able to apply the math you have learned. "They are so used to rote problem solving. Do this and you get that. When we start giving them what math teachers call 'word problems,' they just fall apart. We put everything into word problems because we are tasked to prepare these students for the real worlds. I'd tell [high school students] to do tons of them."

And a physics professor: "Math is the language of physics. Taking calculus, pre-calculus, or trigonometry is really helpful." (He also recommends taking a lab class in high school.)

You have taken every math class offered at your high school, and got an A in every single one. How do you know if you are adequately prepared? The math department has a web site that will help you find out. Go to **www.math.usma.edu** and click on the link "Prospective Students." You can take a sample of the math skills test you will take when you arrive. The site also contains a list of math concepts you should already know. Go over them carefully, and if you find any that you are unsure of, get some extra help from your favorite math teacher.

One other word of advice from a math professor: "If you really want to learn math while you are in high school, make an attempt to help your classmates as much as possible. You always learn something better when you have to teach it or explain it."

OTHER WORDS OF ADVICE FROM PROFESSORS

Part of the challenge is simply making the transition to a college environment. "They're accustomed to being spoon-fed," said a Chemistry professor. "When they come here, they're expected to be prepared, to have studies, to be ready to participate. They have to be ready to ask questions on what they read, talk about problem areas, and be involved in class."

Projects and experiments make academic lessons practical.   *United States Military Academy*

You also have to be mentally prepared to work at a subject that's causing you difficulty. The head of the math department explains, "At some point, you will hit a wall. It's a rude awakening when you suddenly have to work at it. Sometimes you can't get it and want to give up, because you don't know how to work at it."

Being responsible for your own learning means that you have to do the homework. Practice problems and exercises are given so that you and your professor can determine whether you understand the material. Don't move on to something new until you are sure you have learned what was already taught. A math professor said, "I wish I could get them to realize just this one point. If they spend their entire two-hour math homework time working only on what they covered in the last class, they would never be more than one lesson behind."

A chemistry professor explained, "Sometimes we'll give a quiz that is the exact replica of their homework assignment. If you did your homework, you've just earned a sure 100 on the quiz. I you haven't done it, you're either going to get a zero or some low grade because there is no way you will have time to do the quiz if you haven't already done the problems."

Another professor points out that many cadets have trouble with "compartmentalization of learning," meaning they are not prepared to apply what they learn in one class or discipline to another. In high school, you can practice this application by thinking about how your lessons cross over into other classes.

Many professors advise changing your attitude about asking for help. Most cadets succeeded in high school having never gone to a teacher for extra help after school or during a free period. At West Point, additional instruction, or AI, is all part of a day's work. However, the instructors can't make you get AI. You have to ask for it, and you have to get that help quickly or you will get so far behind that you can't catch up.

Getting As means being honest and humble when you are struggling. Most of all, it means realizing that you don't get extra credit for going in alone. There is nothing wrong, and much that is right, about getting help. That is why the professors are there.

A math professor said, "A problem we see all the time is students coming in here with egos that will not allow them to admit they need help. We are all tasked to give 'additional instruction,' or AI. But so many students wait too long to ask for it." Then he told us to "Put this in capital letters: ASKING FOR HELP IS NOT A SIGN OF WEAKNESS." So we did!

CHAPTER 7
Physical Preparation

If you have a preconceived notion about West Point as a physical place — pictures in your mind of road marches, pushups, and hand-to-hand combat drills — your idea is probably correct. The physical and mental stress of combat (and combat training) require all Soldiers to be in top physical condition. At West Point, the physical education department and upperclass cadets hold themselves responsible for creating in all the plebes the foundation of career-long fitness, a responsibility that everyone there takes very seriously. After all, in the end, lives could be at stake.

In 2015, the very first two women Soldiers graduated from the mentally and physically demanding Ranger school, out of 19 who attempted. You should not be surprised to learn that both successful women are West Point grads.

If the thought of physical activity turns you off — activities such as running, calisthenics, obstacle courses, and long hikes — perhaps West Point is not the best choice for you.

On the other hand, if you enjoy physical activity, competition, pushing yourself to new limits in new physical skills and activities, you'll have a head start at West Point. Even better, you will have leading edge facilities and equipment, plus highly trained and educated staff to help you improve.

And if you are somewhere in between? You need to come to terms with the fact that as a cadet, nearly every day will involve some physical activity. As with the academic and military obligations at West Point, anything you can do ahead of time to make the physical demands easier will help you tremendously.

If you show up in poor physical condition, chances are, through hard work and extra effort, others will help you improve and meet standards over time. But not a single cadet, graduate, or PE instructor recommends this approach. Why not? If you show up on R-day and aren't in the best physical condition, what will happen? Three things. First, you will be more drained by the physical challenges than your more fit classmates. As a result, you will be more tired and less able to concentrate, and you will probably lose some confidence, which is a precious commodity for new cadets and plebes.

Second, you will lose credibility. Everyone will expect you to keep up physically. You will have to prove your strength and endurance to your classmates and the upperclassmen every day. If you fail to complete a road march or other physical task, your entire team fails. The respect of the other cadets, including your classmates, will depend in part on your physical performance. If you even appear to be weak or lazy, you will have to work that much harder to regain that respect.

Third, you could fail the graded physical fitness tests or PE classes. This failure incurs extra conditioning and training, which means extra time…the most valuable and scarce asset a cadet has.

You should make a commitment that when you show up at West Point on R-day, you will be in superb physical condition. How will you know if you are ready?

HOW TO GET IN SHAPE

The Academy has a detailed program to help you get in shape before you even arrive for CBT. This program can be found on the candidates admissions page under Personal Fitness Tracker (once you become a candidate you will have an account and log-in access to this site). When you receive an appointment offer, you will also receive a 15-page packet with very specific training advice. If you do not have access to a gym, don't be discouraged — it isn't necessary.

The recommended program focuses on both aerobic fitness and strength training. For starters, you should be able to run four miles in 32 minutes or less. The physical education department also recommends incorporating interval training and other aerobic activities to increase your endurance.

You should also do road marches to toughen your feet and build endurance, working up to eight miles at about three miles per hour with a 25 pound load. Break in a pair of combat boots (available at any Army surplus store, do NOT use jungle boots or paratrooper "jump" boots) and a good pair of running shoes so you don't get blisters.

Strength training focuses on old-fashioned situps and pushups. By doing a regular routine of situps and pushups every other day, you can build enough strength to pass the Army Physical Fitness Test. Pullups are also good for building strength, so it's worth the investment to install a pullup bar somewhere in your house as you prepare. Rope climbing or any other exercise that builds upper body strength will also be helpful.

If you are a competitive, varsity athlete, you may think that your sport has made you more than fit enough for West Point. That isn't necessarily true, PE instructors say. Because athletics are so specialized, you may have the strength to do one kind of physical activity and not others. For example, if you are a cross country runner or a soccer player, are you also working on upper body strength? Even athletes should evaluate their overall fitness carefully before they arrive at West Point.

You will definitely be evaluated at West Point, probably within a day or two of arriving. The first test will require you to do two minutes of pushups, two minutes of situps, and a two-mile run (with short rest breaks in between the three events). You will be retested at the end of CBT. According to the director of the PE department (traditionally known as "The Master of the Sword"), about 47% of new cadets fail the first test. This test tends to be a real eye-opener for young men and women who considered themselves in good shape. Those who fail will receive extra help over the summer, and by the end of CBT, typically less than 10% will fail the retest.

WHAT TO EXPECT

Physical training will be a big part of every day during CBT. New cadets do group physical

Expect to be challenged physically every day.   *United States Military Academy*

training from 5:30 to 7:00 each morning, including group runs and calisthenics. Sometimes you will do "guerrilla drills," involving bear crawls and crab walks in the grass. New cadets also participate in a warrior competition in squad-sized units, trying to outdo the other companies in activities such as an obstacle course, a wall scale, pugil stick training, a bayonet assault course, and an agility course.

Road marches begin during CBT, starting with a three-mile march wearing a helmet and harness, and culminating with a 15-mile march wearing a pack and carrying a weapon. If you do not complete each march, you may not pass CBT. More importantly, your classmates will remember you as someone who can't pull their own weight.

Eventually CBT ends, you officially become a plebe, and the academic year starts. Then the physical demands let up, right? Wrong. You will be continually challenged and assessed throughout your four years as a cadet.

All cadets must take the Army Physical Fitness Test eight times, in the fall and spring each year. Details and standards for this test are available at **armyenlist.com**. Cadets are expected to exceed the Army standards — getting a 100% based on the Army requirements will earn cadets a grade of A-. Those who fail to meet the basic Army standards twice will enter a 90-day remediation program, and then retest. Another failure can result in dismissal from West Point. In fact, 10-15 cadets per year will leave for failing to meet APFT standards.

Many of the PE classes are very demanding as well. Your PE classes will depend on your individual abilities. For example, during CBT you will complete a 150 yard timed swim to assess your swimming skill. Based on the results, you will be placed in a swimming course from remedial to advanced. Ultimately, you will have to pass a survival swimming course.

Another challenging course is Military Movement, or applied gymnastics —

During CBT, you will run and run, then run some more.   *United States Military Academy*

affectionately called spaz-nastics by cadets. According to the head of the PE department, "With today's specialized sports, video games, supersized fast food, and not playing outside as they are growing up, many cadets come in without the broad movement background they need in the Army." About 50 to 80 cadets fail this course each year, which means they have to retake it — another activity added to an already-full schedule.

To ensure you are ready to contribute to the Army's deployed, combat mission, West Point has created a new graduation requirement. In February of your junior year, you will have to pass an indoor obstacle course, a "functional test for the Army." This course includes a low crawl, vault, tires, rope climb, running with a load, scaling a wall, and a balance beam. During the Military Movement class you take during plebe year, you will have the opportunity to practice this course.

On top of all this, during the afternoons after classes are over, you will have more physical activity. Intercollegiate athletes will head off to their practices. The rest of the Corps will participate in intramural sports competitions every other day. The other afternoons may be spent studying, marching in parades, or going on runs or road marches with their platoons.

If you want to find out more about physical training, testing, and education at West Point, we recommend you explore the department's web site: **http://www.usma.edu/dpe/**.

You can see that West Point will stretch you to your limits physically, even if you were a good athlete in high school. These demands will be easier if you are prepared, both mentally and physically, for all you will have to do.

Some final thoughts from the PE department head: "Take the literature we send you to heart, and do it. If you come in as physically prepared as possible, there's one less thing on a demanding plate. It can be hot and humid and you'll get run down. But the more fit you are, the better you can weather that in terms of stamina.

"The Army is a land-based, physical culture. At the end of the day, we need Soldiers on the ground to hold terrain and complete tasks that require a high degree of physicality in a tough environment. Being a Soldier requires a higher-than-average degree of fitness from everyone so the Army can accomplish the mission. You have to commit early on to improve every day. It's leadership by physical example."

CHAPTER 8

Other Preparation

You have heard how academically challenging West Point is for most cadets. You know you need good test scores and grades to be competitive for an appointment. You have read about the physical requirements, the need to be physically fit. But being a scholar and an athlete, even being outstanding at both, isn't enough! You must also prove that you have developed other skills, and that you have the ability to become someone who can lead men and women in combat.

EXTRACURRICULAR ACTIVITIES = LEADERSHIP POTENTIAL

The Army needs leaders, and you must prove that you have the potential to be one of those leaders. How do you do that?

In high school, you have many opportunities outside the classroom to use and develop your capabilities. Examples include team sports, clubs, student government, newspaper and yearbook staffs, drama, band, drill team, chorus and debate.

They also may include activities outside of school such as Explorer and Eagle Scouts, church and community volunteer service, Civil Air Patrol, Junior ROTC, and service organizations.

Extra-curricular activities (or ECA) are important for those who want to go to the Academy because participation demonstrates the qualities that are valuable at the Academy and in the Army. For example, a student who has played football or run on a cross-country team has experienced hardships, learned self-sacrifice and developed mental toughness. Also, such a student has learned the value of teamwork and has developed a competitive attitude.

Participation in ECA demonstrates that candidates are not selfish with their time — that they have a desire to serve. The desire to serve others is an essential part of an officer's makeup. Above all, you are going to West Point to enter the military service. Those who are self-centered and selfish with their time are better suited for other careers.

The ability to get along with people and motivate them is another essential trait for an Army officer. When a candidate can demonstrate ECA leadership experience, that is a strong indicator of officer potential. To those who evaluate candidates, it is far better to have been the elected president of one club than to be simply a member of three. Likewise, it is better to have been a team captain, a newspaper editor or student council president than to have been just a member of those groups.

A student who has held leadership positions has learned something else that is considered valuable by those who evaluate candidates, a skill all successful cadets must possess: time management.

At the Academy there is never enough time to do all the things that are supposed to be done. In order to survive, the cadet has to compromise and prioritize. Some things have to be left undone and others have to be done in their order of importance. Cadets have to find time for relaxation and recreation, without letting their play get in the way of their work. That is the art of time management we have been talking about.

High school students who take hard academic classes and hold ECA leadership positions have had to learn some of those time management skills. A candidate who is both a scholar and a leader is considered to be better prepared for the rigors of the Academy than one who has never been pressured for time.

In addition to ECA, work experiences also are considered important by some persons who evaluate candidates. For example, several panelists who serve on congressional screening committees have flatly stated that they prefer candidates who have had real-world work experiences.

Why? For most panelists, their main goal is to evaluate the motivation and potential dedication of the candidates who come before them. Some panelists believe that students who have worked at summer jobs or at part-time jobs while attending school are more likely to have the kind of motivation and dedication that is needed to survive at the Academy.

Others see work experiences as just one more opportunity for the candidate to learn to time management. And candidates who have to work to help support their family will impress the panel as young men and women who can handle responsibility.

Certainly, while being interviewed by a panel, if you are asked what you have done during your last two summer vacations, the interrogator is not likely to be impressed if you answer, "I spent my last two summers having fun." You won't get points for being a slacker, even honesty points.

Junior ROTC or any extracurricular activities with a military focus are especially valuable. These ECA provide candidates with opportunities to learn about military culture and traditions, practice leadership, and gain exposure to people with experience serving in the military. Participation in JROTC also shows that you are seriously committed to serving in the military. Similarly, participation in Boy Scout and Girl Scout leadership positions is highly regarded, especially if you earn your Eagle Scout or Gold Award.

GET A HEAD START

Some other types of preparation for the Academy are not essential for getting admitted. However, there are things a candidate can do prior to enrollment that will make life at the Academy much easier once you are there.

The first concerns various kinds of knowledge. As soon as Plebe Summer begins, the new plebe is required to learn about West Point and Army history, the structure and composition of the Army, and a very long list of other facts. All of these are contained in a little book called Bugle Notes, which is issued to each plebe. If memorizing is not your strong suit, you can make it easier on yourself by memorizing, or at least familiarizing yourself with much of the material in that book. You can find an upperclassman or Academy graduate and borrow a copy, or find one to purchase online.

Some cadets and graduates advise you not to worry about getting a head start on this memorization. But if the Army is a completely alien world to you, the transition will be easier if you spend a little time online or at the library learning about the Army — its branches, rank structure, and history.

Plebes are also expected to read the daily newspaper and keep up with current events. It is recommended that you start this habit several months before going to the Academy. It is a good habit and it will help you to have the background and perspective for what you will read about later.

You can also give your feet a head start by breaking in a pair of combat boots, black leather dress shoes (not patent leather) and a pair of running shoes. You can order boots and dress shoes online, or the Academy will provide you with authorization to go to a military base and purchase them. A MALO recommends the latter option if possible, so you can try them on. He also recommends using lots of saddle soap and polish to get them soft, because "if your feet are not happy, you will not be happy." If you can learn how to polish shoes (and brass), you'll save some time. Your running shoes should look fairly low key, rather than neon yellow or hot pink, so you do not get any extra attention during CBT. Standing out from the crowd is not appreciated during Beast.

SEE FOR YOURSELF

Another recommendation — one that is given enthusiastically by nearly everyone who knows anything about the Academy — is to make a personal visit and see for yourself what the Academy experience is all about. There are a several good ways to go about this.

The best way is to participate in the Summer Leaders Experience. You can apply on line starting in December of your junior year by going to the admissions web site and clicking on Summer Program. Part of the application process for Summer Leaders Experience is completing a Candidate Questionnaire. So when you apply to SLS, you have also begun the application process for the Academy (see Chapter 9).

Summer Leaders Experience provides you with a taste of Academy life, including academic, military, and physical training. According to the director of admissions, it will give you "an up close and personal view of the Academy." SLE does not attempt to replicate Academy life, but will give you the chance to experience leadership challenges in a structured and slightly stressful military environment. You will interact with upperclass cadets and professors, including some recent graduates with combat experience.

How do you get selected for Summer Leaders Experience? SLE is almost as competitive as getting into West Point, offering about 1,000 slots for 6,000 applicants each summer. Your test scores (PSAT, SAT, or ACT), grade point average, and class ranking will be considered. Historically, about half of SLE attendees go on to receive and accept appointments to the Academy. The cost of the program is currently $400, which includes room, meals, and training materials. You will also have to pay the cost of your travel.

If you do not participate in Summer Leaders Experience, the Academy offers half-day admissions tours every weekday but Wednesday. Go to the admissions web site and click on Visit West Point to find out more and set up your tour.

You can also participate in a sports camp. The Academy offers week-long camps in a dozen different sports for kids age 10 and up. While you will not experience Academy

Summer Leaders Experience is a great way to see if West Point is right for you.

United States Military Academy

life directly, you will have the opportunity to see the barracks and other facilities up close, and perhaps interact with some cadets. If you attend a sports camp, you will have to pay the cost of registration and travel. More information is available at **www.goarmysports.com** (click on Camps).

Finally, if you receive an offer of appointment, you may participate in a candidate orientation. The visits are a day and a half long, during the week. You will have a cadet escort who will take you to classes, meals, and the barracks where you will spend the night in a cadet room.

What if you cannot visit the Academy? You may not be able to take time away from your job or other activities. You may live too far away and be unable to afford the travel expenses. Will the fact that you have never visited count against you in the admissions process?

No. If you live in Albany, about an hour away from West Point, a nomination panel would be surprised if you never took the time to see the Academy up close. But if you live in Alaska, do all your other homework, and become as informed as you can about the Academy and the Army…everyone will understand why you have not visited.

So far this book has described some of the challenges you will face if you go to the Academy, tips for preparing yourself, and a chance to review your personal motivation for wanting to apply. Do you still think you want to be a cadet? If so, read the next section very carefully. The next chapters describe how to navigate a complex and competitive admissions process that will eliminate about 90 percent of your competition.

HOW TO GET IN

CHAPTER 9

Applying to the Academy: Getting Started

Getting into the U.S. Military Academy is not an easy process. There are letters to write, forms to complete, a medical examination, a physical fitness test, letters of recommendation to solicit and perhaps several interviews. In addition there are deadlines to be met and appointments to be kept.

If you are serious about going to the Academy, you should be happy that the process is so involved. Why? Because the complexity of the process helps eliminate much of your competition.

When faced with all the forms and letters, many students give up immediately. Others start the process but are careless, either with the forms, the deadlines, or the appointments they make. They eliminate themselves. Every competitor who is eliminated helps your chances — if you are determined to do the process correctly.

And you must realize there is a lot of competition. Each year, about 11,000 people begin the application process. Out of the initial applicants there may be nearly 2,000 who complete the process, secure a nomination and are found fully qualified. Yet there are only about 1,300 openings each year!

In ski racing, the difference between the winner of a race and those who finish second, third and fourth may be just hundredths of a second. Much the same concept applies to competition among fully qualified Academy candidates.

Fractions of one point often separate those who get in and those who do not. But you should not be discouraged by this. You should look at it as good news because you can gain points in the admissions process IF you know what to do and what NOT to do.

So here is some advice on the first steps of the admissions process — advice from a variety of sources, including Academy officials, Congressional staff members, field force officers, high school counselors and cadets who retain vivid memories of their own experiences.

GETTING STARTED: THE SOONER THE BETTER

The first step is to determine if you are eligible for the Academy or will be eligible at some future date. Here are the requirements:
- Be at least 17 years old.
- Not yet have passed your 23rd birthday on July 1st of the year you will enter the Academy
- Be a U.S. citizen by the time you enter the Academy (international students authorized admission are exempt from the U.S. citizenship requirement)

• Be of high moral character
• Meet high leadership, academic, physical, and medical standards.
• Be unmarried, not pregnant, with no dependents (including dependent parents)

Your next step, if you think you can meet the above requirements, is to visit the Admissions web site, **www.westpoint.edu/admissions**. The web site contains the most up-to-date information on the admissions process, as well as general information on such things as the curriculum and types of majors that are available. The site is very thorough and contains more information than this section of our book — spend plenty of time looking through it. We also recommend you print out the application timeline and post it somewhere very visible!

Note that you must complete a Candidate Questionnaire as a first step. You can complete the Candidate Questionnaire on line after December 15th of your junior year.

All those who are involved in the admissions procedure recommend that you START EARLY. During your sophomore year you should ask your counselor for the dates when the Preliminary Scholastic Aptitude Test (PSAT) and Preliminary American College Test (PACT) can be taken.

Take one of them and, if you can afford it, take both — and take them as many times as you can. Experience with these tests will almost surely help you later when the regular tests are taken.

During your junior year take the regular SAT or ACT tests as soon as you can and repeat them if you can afford it. The Academy will accept your BEST scores.[1] The LATEST you should take either the SAT or ACT for the first time is June following your junior year.

If you take them later, you will probably not have the scores back in time for the deadlines imposed by your nomination sources. Most Congressional offices require all applications to be complete in October or November of the year you are applying.

Work closely with your school counselor during all phases of the application process. Experienced counselors have usually been through the admissions process several times with other students. Some have visited the Academy on special orientation programs.

MILITARY ACADEMY LIAISON OFFICERS

Also, you will meet with your military academy liaison officer, or MALO. MALOs, also known as Field Force Officers, are Army Reserve officers and civilians who are parents, retired officers, graduates, counselors, anyone who wants to help young people become cadets. There are 700 MALOs, with at least a few in every state. If you live in an area with a large military population, chances are you have a MALO close by. If not, your MALO may live hundreds of miles away, but he or she will be accessible via email and phone. Because many MALOs must cover a large amount of territory and a large number of high schools, you may not meet in person until after you have a congressional nomination.

---

[1]They will take your best verbal and math scores from different SATs. For example, if on the first try you get a 680 Verbal and a 650 Math score, and on the second try you get a 660 Verbal and a 670 Math, they will credit you with a 680 Verbal and 670 Math score for a total of 1350.

How do you find your MALO? Your school counselor or JROTC instructor may know who he or she is. If not, call the admissions office at 845-938-5705 to find out or go to the admissions page's contact us to find the locator map.

Then what? Telephone, email, or write your MALO just to touch base and get acquainted. Your MALO can answer your questions, discuss what an officer's life is like or, if you are more seriously interested, counsel you about preparation or admissions. Your MALO can also connect you with cadets who are home on recruiting visits, or events such as service academy days presented by congressional offices.

MALOs also have an important role in the selection process. They evaluate each candidate in their district, after a one-on-one interview and a reviewing of the candidate's records. Their evaluation is very important because their report tells the admissions board about your motivation, attitude, and potential.

Once you are further along the application process, your MALO will conduct a personal interview with you.

This interview is very important, for two reasons. First, MALOs will make sure you understand what you are getting into as a cadet. They can answer questions and give you advice about getting in and surviving. You will probably enjoy talking with them.

But make no mistake, you are also being evaluated. As one explained, "My job is to put eyeballs on candidates and vet them. I look at their initiative, how they carry themselves, how they express themselves, and what questions they have. My main focus is their motivations. Are they interested in serving in the Army? I can tell early on in the conversation where they're coming from."

In other words, if you are applying because your mother or father or uncle wanted you to, the MALO will sniff that out…and advise you not to bother.

After the interview, the MALO writes a report and mails it to the admissions office. A good interview with your MALO will not move you to the front of the line, but a bad one can move you to the back. They say, "I can't get them in, but I can keep them out."

In order to be prepared before your meeting with your MALO, study the admissions web site and learn as much as you can about the Academy. That way you can ask specific questions, which demonstrates that you are interested enough to have spent time investigating. They know how much information is available on line. At the very least, make yourself very familiar with the admissions web site. Everyone in the admissions process expects you to do what you need to do with minimal help.

The MALO will also see how quickly candidates complete their paperwork, a clear sign of evaluate how motivated they are. They will tell you that the sooner you get started, the better. Said a Nebraska MALO, "Tell them, 'Start early, start early, start early.'"

ARE YOU QUALIFIED?

How does the Academy decide who is qualified and who is not? The web site has many of the details, and you should study it carefully. But here is a brief summary. Each eligible candidate who meets all physical requirements is evaluated on three general criteria.

Are you medically qualified? The Academy graduates officers to lead in the operational Army. They must be able to withstand the physical demands of a combat environment, and may be deployed in austere conditions where medical care is very limited. Poor eyesight, including color blindness, is a common reason for medical disqualification.

What if you are told you are not medically qualified? Is your dream of attending the Academy over just like that? Many medical conditions that are disqualifying at the first look are often waiverable after further review. If you had some childhood disease or other condition that resulted in the initial "no" answer, but that condition does not affect your life now, you may still be able to attend. It is worth your trouble to request a medical waiver.

The most important criterion for admission, other than physical qualification, is academic potential. This is determined by the candidate's grades, rank in class, college courses completed (if applicable) and SAT or ACT scores. In a recent Academy class, 68 percent of the cadets graduated in the top 20 percent of their high school class. Their average SAT verbal and math scores were both over 600.[2]

Another important factor for admissions is the candidate's extracurricular activities, because they tell the admissions board about your leadership potential and your ability to juggle multiple responsibilities. These include school activities such as athletics, clubs and student government and also community activities such as scouting, JROTC, and church activities. The admissions board is also interested in your summer and academic-year work experiences.[3] More points are awarded for leadership roles than for simple membership. A recent entering class included more than 700 National Honor Society members, 222 student government presidents, and 708 athletic team captains.

The final consideration is the MALO's assessment based on the interview.

ADMISSIONS ADVICE

Many candidates make costly mistakes in the admissions process — mistakes that hurt their chances of getting into the Academy. Most of these are easily avoided. Here is how.

1. Be Thorough with All Things

"My pet peeve," said a Congressional staffer, "is the candidate who leaves empty blanks in a form. Then, when I ask the person why, I get a dumb answer like, 'Oh, my coach is going to write a letter telling you all that stuff.'"

The above incident is one example of how candidates hurt themselves by not being thorough. Another is when the candidate says, after all his paperwork has been submitted, "Oh, I forgot to put down the summer job I had at Burger King between my sophomore and junior years." How do you think such carelessness might be interpreted?

Before you even start the application process, create a file listing all your achievements. Organize them into categories such as academics, sports, community service, and clubs. Remember to include every job, activity, award and volunteer effort — student

---

[2] ACT scores averaged 28 in both English and math.
[3] Candidates who have to work to supplement family income often have limited opportunity for club or sport involvement. The board understands this situation and will not penalize the candidate for their lack of extracurricular activities; the candidate is showing the ability to handle responsibility by holding a job and helping to care for his or her family.

of the month, head of the charity clothing drive, team co-captain, or bus boy at the local restaurant. It all shows your ability to take on added responsibility and stand out above the average high school student.

It might feel like bragging, but you have to tell the admissions board why you are Academy material. Do not rely on others to sell you — no one knows all you have accomplished as well as you, and no one else cares about your application as much.

2. Be Neat

"Can you believe that I get letters and forms in here that are dirty or have coffee stains on them?" sighed a Congressional staffer. That was one of many complaints heard from those who must deal with candidate forms and letters.

Neatness is a habit that WILL be learned if the candidate ever gets into the Academy. But those who deal with candidates generally look more highly at those who already demonstrate such habits. Give yourself every chance to be one of those who are thought of in that way.

Be neat. Be neat with your paperwork. And be neat with your appearance — neat hair, shoes, and clothes make an impression on everyone, especially those with a military background.

3. Always Be On Time or, Better, Be Early

What is your opinion of the following three candidates? All three say they have a strong desire to go to the Academy. But one of them shows up ten minutes early for an interview, the other just exactly at the minute the interview is to start, and the third shows up five minutes late.

Are you likely to think that the first candidate, the one who showed up early, has the most desire? That is the way most evaluators think. So pay attention to deadlines. Get your paperwork in on time — if you cannot get it in early. Get to your appointments on time — if you cannot get to them early. NEVER BE LATE WITH ANYTHING IF YOU CAN HELP IT.

One Naval Academy blue and gold officer (their equivalent of a MALO) mentioned that nearly every November, he gets a call or an e-mail from a candidate asking about the congressional nomination process. The answer by that point is, "It's too late now." His advice: Pay close attention to all deadlines. A West Point MALO echoed this recommendation, pointing out that some congressional offices have deadlines as early as August, so if you wait to get going until you're in the routine of your senior year at school, it may be too late. "They have firm cutoff dates. And if you don't have a nomination, you're going nowhere."

4. Check All Grammar, Punctuation and Spelling

Everyone will make mistakes when filling out forms or writing letters. The important thing is to CATCH those mistakes before they go out and tell the world that you use poor grammar, cannot punctuate, or cannot spell.

There is no reason for a candidate to submit forms or letters with mistakes. To prevent this from happening, do two things.

First, write out the answers on a separate sheet of paper or hit "Print Screen" to create a hard copy of on-line forms. Second, ask your counselor, English teacher or some other qualified person to read your forms and letters to make sure there are no mistakes in grammar, punctuation or spelling. Just checking them yourself is not enough.

When you are filling out forms on line, it is very easy to hit "submit" before you have thoroughly reviewed all your responses. But there is too much at stake for you to take a chance. Review every entry for accuracy. Remember, there is nothing wrong with asking for help. After all, professional writers do the same thing. They submit their work to editors who check what they have written before it ends up in print and possibly embarrasses them.

5.   Always Remember, You, and Not Your Parents, are Applying to the Academy
Consider this situation: A MALO shows up to interview Johnny at his house, and Johnny's father, who served for twenty years in the Army, does all the talking and asks all the questions while Johnny looks at his shoes. Then Johnny's mother appears more interested than Johnny in how to fill out the on-line application or get a congressional nomination.

Maybe Johnny's mother and father, not Johnny, think he should go to the Academy. Parents can provide wonderful support for candidates during the admissions process, and later if the candidate becomes a cadet. But there is a big difference between support and ACTIVE INVOLVEMENT. Everyone participating in the admissions process is deeply wary of parents who appear to hover like a helicopter over their son or daughter's candidacy. The tragedies of cadets who were pushed into the Academy by overzealous parents are well known. Every person who evaluates a candidate will be looking for that kind of parent over-involvement and SCREEN OUT that candidate.

One MALO explained all the negative consequences of going to West Point for the wrong reasons: "At the Academy, everything comes at you hard and fast. If you aren't personally motivated, you won't make it through. You'll start to feel sorry for yourself and quit. That's baggage you'll carry with you all your life."

So, take charge of your own admissions requirements. Do not rely on your parents to do the work for you or let the process get out of your control. Make all calls YOURSELF. Look upon each call you must make not as a chore, but as another opportunity to sell yourself. If your parents insist on helping, ask them to read Chapter 24. It is written just for them.

APPLY TO OTHER ACADEMIES AND ROTC

You might think it odd that applying to other schools would make help you get into the Academy. But remember, MALOs and congressional nomination panels are interested in why you want to attend the Academy.

They are looking for young men and women who want to serve their country. If you are truly committed to that goal, it makes sense that you would pursue every possible path, including other service academies and ROTC programs at civilian colleges. Why would they believe in the motivation of a candidate who has made no effort to come up with an alternate plan for becoming an officer?

As a Navy blue and gold officer explained, "If I have to tell a kid to apply to ROTC, I'm not going to rank him very high. Why do you want to go to the Naval Academy? I need to hear about service to country, so if you are serious about serving, you should look at all the options. I believe I'm recruiting for the country, not just the Naval Academy."

Many MALOs will advise you to apply to all of the academies. For one thing, it shows you are serious about serving in the military. Also, you may get an appointment to all the academies, and then have your choice. And if you get selected for Navy and only wanted West Point, you can always decide to turn it down. However, if you are 100% certain that Army is your first or only choice, say so.

Regardless, make sure you have a reasonable back-up plan. Applying to other schools shows initiative and drive, and that you think ahead and are mature enough to realize that life does not always turn out as you would like. These are all traits that will serve you well if you do get into the Academy.

If you follow all these tips, you will make a positive impression on your MALO. You will also have the right frame of mind for embarking on the process of getting a nomination. The nomination is extremely important, because you cannot get an appointment without one — which is why it is the subject of the next three chapters.

Chapter 10

The Second Step: Getting the Nomination

Sometime during the second half of your junior year is when you officially begin the application process by filling out your Candidate Questionnaire. It is also a good time to begin your quest for a nomination.

But the procedure is much more involved than the application process. In seeking a nomination you should probably make separate applications to at least four different nomination sources. Your four primary sources are the two U.S. Senators from your state, the U.S. Representative from your congressional district and the U.S. Vice President. In this book, U.S. Senators and U.S. Representatives will be called "congressmen" and their nominations will be called "congressional nominations."

You may also be eligible for a number of other nominations if you fit one of these categories:
- Children of active duty or retired military
- Children of deceased or disabled veterans
- Children of Medal of Honor recipients
- Active duty, guard and reserve enlisted personnel
- ROTC and JROTC midshipmen and cadets

The simplest of all the applications is the one to the Vice President. This nomination is also the hardest to get since there are only one or two are available each year for the whole United States. A sample letter is available on the Academy admissions web site, and more information is available by clicking on the "Learn More" link at the bottom of the page on **www.whitehouse.gov/vicepresident**.

Getting a congressional nomination can be a lot more complicated because of the paperwork required. Also, many congressmen require that candidates go before a panel to be interviewed and evaluated.

Many states now hold annual Service Academy Information Days, where staffers from the congressional offices, liaison officers, parents clubs, cadets and midshipmen, and graduates make themselves available in one location to talk to prospective candidates. They will answer questions and give you resources and advice on the admissions process. Your school counselor, MALO, or congressional staffer can tell you about if these opportunities exist in your state.

But what about politics? Do your parents have to have political "pull" for you to obtain a congressional nomination? Many people believe that to be true. Some believe that your parents have to belong to the same political party as the congressman. Others believe that your parents or relatives have to have helped in the congressman's campaign or contributed money to it.

In fact, a 2014 U.S. News article tried to make that argument, and the only evidence they could cite was a few small past campaign donations by candidates' families, and no real link to the process. The article also criticized the fact that each member of Congress could design his or her own process and criteria — that is true, but it certainly doesn't make the nomination process corrupt or even political.

Years ago some of those beliefs may have been true — service academy nominations were sometimes awarded as political favors. However, according to hundreds who have been interviewed for the books in this candidate series, the role of politics is relatively unimportant now. As a MALO explained, "The congressmen want to appear fair and impartial." Also, congressmen do not want to waste their constituents' tax dollars paying for the wrong candidate to attend the Academy. They want to make sure the candidates with the best records and the best chance for success receive nominations.

NOMINATION MATH

There are a total of 535 congressmen — 435 representatives and 100 senators. Each has a quota of five cadets or midshipmen who can be at each service academy at any given time. Thus, each year there is usually at least one upcoming vacancy because at least one of the five will probably be graduating. For each vacancy, the congressman can make ten nominations.

Do not let all those numbers confuse you. Just remember that for each vacancy, the congressman is entitled to submit a list of ten nominees from his state or district.

There are three ways the congressman can list those ten nominees when he or she submits the list.

By far the most common method is to make what is called a competitive list. By this method the congressman gives all the names on the list equal ranking. By doing it this way the congressman is telling the Admissions Office, "I have screened the candidates in my state/district and here are the ten who I think are the best. Now it is up to you to decide which candidates should be offered an appointment."

The second method is the principal/alternate method. By this method the congressman picks one nominee to get a principal nomination. This principal nominee, if fully qualified, must be offered an appointment to the Academy first, before any of the alternates on the list can be appointed. And if any of the alternates, which are ranked in sequence — first alternate, second alternate, third alternate, etc. — are appointed, they must be appointed according to their ranking if they are fully qualified.

The third method, which is the principal/competitive method, is a combination of the previous two. The congressman makes one nominee the principal nominee, but the nine alternates are competitive. The Academy can then decide who, if any, should be appointed from the list of alternates.

Admissions officials will pick one nominee from the congressman's list, either the principal nominee or the most qualified nominee if it is a competitive list. That nominee will be offered an appointment. If he or she accepts the appointment, that person is the one who will count against the congressman's quota of five who can be at the Academy at any one time.

However, the Academy usually offers appointments to others who are on the congressman's list of ten. Those who accept are not charged against the congressman's quota. So, even though each congressman has a theoretical quota of five who can be at the Academy at any one time, it is not unusual for one congressman to actually have more than 10 and sometimes as high as 20 or more at a service academy at any one time.

And for you, the candidate, that is good news. It means that even though your three congressmen might only have three vacancies the year you apply, your chances of getting an appointment are greatly increased because of all the alternates who are also offered appointments. Three congressmen with a combined quota of three vacancies could easily end up with 10-15 of their nominees being offered appointments.

Much depends upon the qualifications of the alternates. For example, on Congressman A's list of 10 nominees there might be only one who is highly qualified and in that case only the one might be offered an appointment.

But on Congressman B's list there might be five who are much more highly qualified than the nine who were left on the list of Congressman A. Therefore, Congressman B might have five of his nominees offered appointments.

Now let us turn to politics again. Suppose a senator or congressman did pay back a political favor and give some young person a nomination. In most cases the list is competitive, so perhaps one name on the list would be there because of politics whereas the other nine are there on the basis of their own merits. Since the list is competitive, which nominees are going to be offered appointments?

Answer: The nominees the Academy believes to be the best qualified. Therefore, if you manage to get yourself on such a list, you do not have to worry about competition from another nominee unless that nominee is better qualified than you. And if the person is better qualified than you, that person would have gotten a nomination without the political favor.

So, if you or your parents are worried about politics being a part of the nomination process, you are better off to forget it. You will be much better off concentrating on what you must do to earn your place on one of those three lists of nominees.

GETTING STARTED ON THE CONGRESSIONAL NOMINATION

The first thing you must do is contact the three congressional offices — the offices of your two U.S. Senators and your U.S. Representative. If your MALO or counselor has not already armed you with this information, go to **www.house.gov** and **www.senate.gov**. If you do not know the names of your congressmen, just click on your state and the site will lead you to the correct contact information.

Then call each congressman's office — use the one closest to where you live — and ask for the name of the "staffer" who handles the service academy nomination process. Most of the time the staffer who does that is in a regional office, not in Washington, D.C.

When you get the staffer on the phone, tell that person you want to apply for a nomination to a service academy — you do not have to specify which one. The staffer will ask you some basic questions such as your age, address, and year of graduation.

In addition, there is a good chance you will be asked to write a letter formally requesting to be considered as a candidate for a nomination — or a letter explaining why you want to go to a service academy. Why would a staffer ask for such a letter? Why not just send out the congressman's packet of application forms and instructions? There are at least two reasons.

First, there is a common problem of young people calling up saying they want to apply for a nomination just on a whim. They think, "Hey, going to West Point sounds like a neat idea. Why not go for it?" Senators in heavily populated states will get well over a thousand people who are serious about getting a nomination. Requiring a letter is one way of eliminating those who are not really serious.

The second reason why staffers may want a letter requires a little more explanation. Staffers know there are parents who, for economic reasons or to enhance their own prestige, want their sons and daughters to go to a service academy. Some push their sons and daughters openly — often it is a plea get a free education and save money.

But more often the pressure is subtle — so subtle in fact, that the young people are not really aware they are being pressured. They are manipulated in such a way that they have begun to think that going to a service academy is their own idea.

In either case, it is the sons and daughters who are going to suffer because the record of those types surviving at any service academy is absolutely disastrous — previous chapters have already discussed this trap. The academies are very tough: tough academically, tough physically and tough mentally. Those who have very strong self-motivation are the ones who survive. Those who have been manipulated into going to an academy by their parents normally do not. So, just as MALOs do, congressional staffers try to use the admissions process to eliminate those who are not really motivated.

DO IT YOURSELF

Staffers say they get many calls from parents wanting to know what a son or daughter has to do to get a nomination. And from the staffers' comments about such calls, the parent might as well be waving a red warning flag in front of the staffer's face. When a parent calls, the immediate question in the mind of the staffer is, "I wonder if this is a parent who is pushing a kid into applying for an academy?"

So, many staffers do what they can to flush out overzealous parents — and to protect young people from the psychological trauma of eventual failure. When a parent calls about a nomination, some staffers will politely ask the parent to have the son or daughter call, saying — to be diplomatic — that there are a number of questions he or she would like to ask the candidate before sending out the congressman's information packet.

Of course, another way to make an end run around an overzealous parent is to require a letter from the candidate. If the candidate is poorly motivated, he or she can procrastinate writing a letter and in this way thwart the parental pressure. At least that is what the staffer is hoping.[1]

Staffers see another warning flag when parents do the calling for you. Succeeding at

[1] A field representative said that he always makes it a point to tell candidates, "Hey, if this is something you really don't want to do but you don't want to hurt your parents, just leave something out of the application that you send to the academy. The academy probably won't call or write you about it and you won't hurt your parents because they will never know that you sabotaged the application."

the Military Academy requires maturity, initiative, commitment, and self-motivation. If you need your parents to get you through the application process, you probably do not have the traits required to succeed in the high-stress environment of the Academy.

Remember that you are being evaluated every time you interact with someone involved with the nomination or admissions process, not just when the application is read or the formal interview is taking place. Take advantage of every opportunity to make yourself known and present yourself well.

ATTENTION TO DETAIL STARTS NOW

After you have called the staffers and perhaps sent in letters that were required, you will receive three separate application packets — one from each congressman.

It is very important that you follow the instructions in each packet exactly, because each congressman has his or her own philosophy and his or her own way of awarding nominations. Almost nothing makes a staffer so angry as when a candidate takes the information from another congressman's packet and duplicates it. Do not give the staffer the impression that you are not serious enough to pay attention to the smallest details.

So take each packet and keep your materials for each congressman in three separate files. Also, make copies of everything that you submit, marking on each one of them the submission date, and keep those copies in the three separate files. That way you have a record of everything. You will know what has been sent to whom, and when it was sent. If you would consider going to Naval Academy, the Air Force Academy, or the Merchant Marine Academy, be sure to mention that. Give your order of preference; you may receive nominations to more than one academy.

Almost every member of Congress (and also the Admissions Office) will require that you solicit letters of recommendation. Here are some dos and don'ts that will help you get the best possible recommendations.

Do not just walk up to a person from whom you would like to have a letter and ask, "Mr. ___, I'm applying for; will you write a letter of recommendation for me?"

Instead, tell the person you want the letter from that you are thinking of applying to the Military Academy and you are wondering what that person thinks about the idea. This way you get a chance to feel out the person to see if he or she thinks it is a good idea. Perhaps that person will hedge a bit and wonder if you have what it takes for such a challenge. Or, that person might have a strong anti-military bias and feel that you would be wasting your ability going to a service academy. However, another person might be very enthusiastic and think your idea is wonderful.

Which person do you want writing a letter of recommendation for you — the person who is hedging or the person who is enthusiastic about you? The latter, of course. Find out if the person is solidly behind you, then ask for the letter of recommendation. The competition is tough enough already. You certainly do not want any half-hearted letters of recommendation in your file.

When a person has agreed to write a letter for you, you should give that person three things:

1) A self-addressed, stamped envelope for each letter that has to be submitted. Typically, each person will be writing letters to all three members of Congress and perhaps the Admission Office, too.

2) A written deadline that is at least two weeks before the actual deadline. Why? Because the person you ask may be very busy and might forget the deadline or forget to write the letter. Then there are those who are procrastinators — they keep putting it off. (According to congressional staffers, high school principals are the worst procrastinators of all.) By giving an early deadline you can check to see if the letters have arrived and if they have not, you will have time to prod the letter-writers and still make the real deadline.

3) A print out of the file you made recording all of your school and out-of-school activities, awards, elected offices, test scores, community work, part time jobs — and anything else a person writing a letter needs to know about you. Why? Because that person wants to write the best letter possible (you hope) and to do that he or she needs to know all the facts about you. It would be the rare teacher, counselor or principal who knows all of your achievements, even though you may have been in the same school together for four years. So do not take any chances. Give them plenty of ammunition so they can fire their best shots.

Then what?

There is much more advice that could be given, but it will perhaps mean more to you if it is given in the words of some of the 40-odd staffers who were interviewed by the authors. Their comments are the subject of the next chapter.

CHAPTER 11
Tips from Congressional Staffers

The role of the congressional staffer varies considerably from office to office.

At one extreme are the staffers who, by themselves, review all applications, interview all candidates and then make up the lists of nominees that they present to their congressmen, who usually rubber-stamp the list. Staffers like this are very powerful. They know it — and they will let you know it.

At the other extreme are the staffers who only handle the paperwork while an outside panel or the congressman reviews the applications and makes up the lists of nominees. Staffers like this are strictly paper-shufflers and have no input whatsoever on who does or does not receive a nomination.

Most staffers have a role somewhere in between those two extremes. Many screen the applications and use their own judgment — often supported by objective criteria specified by the congressman — on who should be nominated. They may also sit on panels and help interview candidates, or they may take the ratings of panelists and use them to make lists of nominees for the congressman.

And while most of the latter types will try to pass themselves off to candidates and parents as mere paper-shufflers, do not believe it. It is reasonably safe to say that most staffers have at least some power to decide who does and who does not get a nomination. Most of them have been in this role for years; they have seen it all, and will not hesitate to decide whether you are Academy material or not. So be careful. When you are dealing with a staffer, it is prudent to assume that this is the person who is going to decide whether or not you get a nomination.

Now let's hear from the staffers themselves. Dozens of them were interviewed. Many told of one or more visits to the academies. Most expressed strong feelings about the country's need for high-quality military officers. And most indicated that they were doing everything they could to recruit and nominate the best candidates from their district or state.

SHOW YOUR COMMITMENT

Staffers have some frustrating problems with their candidates. One of these problems is the way some candidates procrastinate.

Said a staffer from Arkansas: "They [the candidates] put things off till the last minute and don't realize that I have responsibilities other than handling academy nominations. We have deadlines to meet, too. When a kid pushes me because he has procrastinated, it is going to affect his overall rating."

And a staffer from Washington State: "Some call you up the night before the deadline and say, 'I don't have my pictures yet,' or 'I can't take my SAT until next week.' Or they bring in their letters, transcript, etc. the day of the review and want me to put the file together. That doesn't reflect good organizational ability. That doesn't show dedication. We are going to be skeptical about such candidates. Will they follow through if they get to an academy? They didn't follow through with us when they were told in September what we would need by the first of December. How are kids like this ever going to make it at one of the academies?"

And a staffer from Iowa: "They should be more timely because I won't even consider anybody who doesn't get their paperwork in on time. How could they be a successful at an academy if they can't do that?"

Another frustrating problem for staffers is candidates who do not follow up and check on their files. They point out that numerous things can be missing from a file. For example, SAT scores could be missing because they were sent to Winslow, AR instead of Winslow, AZ — mistakes like that occur all the time.

Another common problem is that high schools, including those with excellent reputations, often leave essential information like class standing off transcripts that they send out.

"The problem [with not following up]," said a staffer from Arkansas, "is that few of these kids really understand how important it is to stay in contact with us. Often there is something missing from their files and before the cut-off date we used to write or call and tell them about it. Now, because of the volume of applications, we just can't do that. Now we just use what is here and some kids will get hurt simply because they don't follow up to see if anything is missing. Of course, in our instructions we tell them to do that. So if they fail to do it they are not following instructions and in my book the ability to follow instructions has to be at the top of the list when it comes to considering candidates for an academy."

And a staffer from Texas: "What bothers me is that these youngsters put their trust in the people they ask for letters [of recommendation], then they fail in not double-checking with me...and I'm not perfect — something could get lost here or in the mail. But to be quite honest, they are supposed to be mature enough to handle four tough years at an academy...we can't coddle them. I've seen what happens at those academies. I know what these kids are fixing to get into. If they can't get their act together for a few pieces of paper, what are they going to do when they get up there and report to the academies for basic training — how are they going to handle that?"

Candidates who do follow up with staffers almost always leave a good impression.

Said a staffer from Iowa: "We do everything in our Washington, D.C. office, and since I never see any of the kids, it is the contact through the telephone and their letters that we use to help judge them. And one thing we know is that these kids hate to write letters. Therefore, it is really impressive when we get a nice letter or two from a kid checking on his file. Of course, we like them to call, too, but when a kid goes to all the trouble to write a letter, you feel that that kid is really motivated and wants to go [to an academy]."

And a staffer from California: "The bottom line is how much do they really want this thing? If they come to me for an application and for the interview and if that is all, they don't want it. I want them to bug me, to bother me. If they touch base with me, that shows that they want this thing. I remember one young man from a Catholic boys' school where 99 percent of the graduates go to college. Three kids from that school had applied but only one came in to see me on a regular basis. West Point, his first choice, was not interested in him but one day he mentioned that he was also interested in Navy. Right away I got on the phone and called them. I asked if there was any chance for him to get a Naval Academy Foundation scholarship. Now, this year, he is a firstie [senior] and has a nomination to go on to graduate school and get his master's. The point is, he came in and I worked for him. Sometimes the academies call me and say, 'What do you think about this guy or that guy?' I'll tell them, 'This guy, yes, because he comes in and follows up — that other guy hasn't shown up so I don't know."

A staffer who is on your side can really help you.

MORE IS NOT BETTER

Some staffers are bothered by things that other staffers do not seem to mind. An example is when a candidate disobeys instructions and submits more letters of recommendation than were requested. Here are some typical comments:

A staffer from Ohio: "It is really dumb when they submit a whole pile of letters — one had sixteen sent; another had twenty and I was about to kill him! I have to write and acknowledge all of them! We ask for just three and we specify that they should be from persons who know them, who have been in contact with them, know their abilities, know their leadership potential, truly know them as a person. It is not going to impress me that honorable Joe Schmo who knew the kid's parents in the forties writes a letter — I'm not even going to put those kinds of letters in the file — I have to make four sets [for the panel who will interview the candidates] and I'm not going to duplicate all of those. Then there are those from the neighbor and Aunt Tillie that tell what a fine person the boy is. I won't put those letters in. Our panel who reviews them doesn't care if your Aunt Tillie says you are a sweetheart and you mow her lawn. They are looking for leaders, not sweethearts."

And said an Arizona staffer: "You know what I do when the applicant doesn't follow instructions and has a whole batch of letters sent? When I get to the Xerox machine to duplicate the letters for the committee, I take the first three letters, no matter who they are from, and I duplicate them. Those are the only letters that the committee sees and the candidate might be hurt if those aren't the best letters. I'm sorry, but that's the way it is. If the candidates can't follow the simple instructions that we give them, how can they expect to get by [at an academy]."

Some staffers also complained about candidates who try to puff their applications with extraneous material.

Said another Ohio staffer. "We are not impressed with attendance awards or a twenty-page essay on why you will make a good cadet or midshipman. We don't request that and we don't want it. We had one kid who put a whole book together — that and fifty cents would get him a cup of coffee."

PARENTS: KEEP OUT

Parents who want to help their sons and daughters with the nomination process are also a problem — not for staffers — their ability to handle all kinds of people diplomatically is a mandatory skill for their job. Unfortunately, the overzealous parent is a problem for those whom they most want to help: their own son or daughter.

Said a staffer from Arkansas: "I've been at this business for 14 years and if there is one thing I have learned, it is to be leery when parents get involved. When mama and daddy are involved, we immediately get worried. We learned the hard way that those kids [who go because their parents want it] don't last at the academies. It is the ones who do it on their own who survive and graduate. My advice to candidates is to not let their parents run the show — we want to know what the applicant wants or desires — we don't want mama and daddy wanting to put their kids in the academy."

Said a staffer from Nevada: "Leadership is what it is all about and they should be able to demonstrate leadership from the moment they start the application. I am not impressed by the child if his parents call me and say, 'What else does Johnny need for his files?' I always wonder what Johnny can do."

Said another staffer from Ohio: "We get a lot of calls from parents and I'm not saying that is wrong. But, if young people are serious about going to an academy, they should make the calls themselves. They should learn how to do this on their own and they should call again if they have questions. This shows maturity and I will remember a kid like that."

Still another staffer from Ohio was more adamant: "I get these calls all the time. 'My Freddie is interested in going to a service academy' and I say, 'That's fine but let us hear from Freddie.' I guess the initial call is fine, but from then on it should be the kid who calls. And to the kid I would say, 'If you don't have the wherewithal to do things for yourself, you don't belong in an academy.'"

The authors realize that it is not always possible for a candidate to keep his or her parents out of the process. But give it your best effort.

When telephone calls need to be made, you make them.

If you need to visit the congressman's regional office, let a parent drive you if that is necessary, but go inside by yourself.

And by all means, when you go for an interview, do not let your parents accompany you past the door. An Arizona staffer told of one mother who became angry and created a scene because she could not accompany her son into an interview. "Can you believe that?" said the staffer. "How could we dare send a kid like that to an academy when mom is not going to be there to hold his hand?"

THE DO LIST

Most of the staffers' comments you have read have been negative in tone. But they were selected for that purpose because you should know the kinds of things that staffers do not like.

You should also know what kinds of things impress staffers. Thus, it is appropriate to conclude this chapter with a list of these things — some of which have already been mentioned or implied.

Staffers are impressed with candidates who:

• Call them early — say, during the spring of their junior year.

• Are polite and use good manners when speaking over the telephone or when they present themselves in person.

• Are dressed neatly and are well groomed.

• Have done their homework — who know what is on the admissions web site, who have talked with cadets and graduates and who have either visited the Academy or read about it.

• Get their paperwork in early.

• Follow up to see if anything is missing from their applications.

Perhaps most of all, they are impressed by candidates who write them letters. So, if you really want a staffer to remember you, write when you apply for your application. Write follow up letters to let the staffer know what letters of recommendation to expect and, later, to make sure all of them arrived. Then write again before the deadline to make sure everything is complete in your file. Also, as a courtesy, if the staffer has done some favor for you or if you get a nomination, write a thank-you letter.

The staffers will appreciate the letters because they know how much you hated to write them. (Most of the staffers probably hate to write letters, too.) So, they will get the unwritten message in your letters which says: "Please pay special attention to me. I am not just one of your average candidates. I am much more serious and much more determined than the others — that is why I didn't just pick up the phone and call you like the others will do. I wrote those letters because I want you to know how much I want to go to West Point."

Said a staffer from Colorado, "I love this part of my job. I get to work with some really great kids." Be one of those really great kids.

CHAPTER 12
Interviews: Advice from Those Who Conduct Them

When you apply to West Point you will almost certainly be interviewed by a MALO. The MALO's evaluation of your aptitude and attitude bears considerable weight in the overall admissions package. In addition to the interview with the MALO, you also may be interviewed by staffers or panelists appointed by one or more of the three congressmen to which you will apply for a nomination. (It is rare for congressmen themselves to interview candidates.)

In the case of the congressional interviews it is important that you go into them well prepared.

Your first concern should be with the kinds of questions that will be asked. Surprisingly, after interviewing more than 80 staffers and panelists, it appears that most candidates are asked about the same questions. Also there was a great deal of agreement among those queried on the kinds of answers that are rated good and bad by the panelists.

THE QUESTIONS

Your interview may be as short as 15 minutes or as long as an hour. As one staffer put it, "The purpose of the interview is to evaluate the candidate's preparation and motivation. We're trying to decide whether they are ready for that kind of commitment."

Remember, your record must stand on its own — your grades and test scores and extracurricular activities must be competitive. That is not what the interviewers are trying to evaluate. They are trying to assess whether you have the right attitude to succeed at a service academy. Following is a list of the questions that you are most likely to be asked. After each question are comments about good and bad answers.

★ *Why do you wwant to go to a service academy?*

This question is almost certain to be asked. And many panelists said that even though the question is anticipated by most candidates, it is still the one that is most difficult for them to answer.

What panelists want to hear is how you personally feel about going to an academy. They want you to talk about your background, your interests and your goals. They want you to explain how a service academy will fit in with the goals that you have set for yourself. "Personalize your answer," was a statement heard over and over from panelists.

Said an attorney from Pennsylvania: "Part of the problem is that their answers are so predictable. They'll say, 'It is something I have wanted since I was a child.' That doesn't tell me why — it just says that I want it. Or they will say, 'I have read about it somewhere and I've always wanted to do that.' That isn't any more helpful.

"Another predictable but useless reply is, 'I think it would be a challenge.' That doesn't tell me anything, either. I think they have to dig deeper for the answer to this question. They should relate their answer to their own personality — they should personalize it a little more — they have to talk about their goals and ambitions. They have to express their feelings to the extent that they are telling something about themselves. It is these personal kinds of answers that are impressive."

Said another attorney from Pennsylvania: "I like to hear things that indicate a strong motivation and commitment. I like to hear them talk about the Academy and tell what they like about it — what they observed if they went there for a visit...things that show a depth of knowledge, things that show they have made an effort to learn about it.

"I am also impressed when I hear things like, 'It has always been my dream to have a military career because ...,' or 'I know myself well enough to know that I like a disciplined environment,' or 'One of my favorite things to do is to read about battles and wars,' or 'I have grown up hearing my father, a retired officer, and my uncle who spent 30 years in the Marine Corps, telling about their experiences. I liked those stories and I would like the opportunity to experience some of the kinds of things they experienced' — those are the statements that show motivation on the part of the kid; they show that the kid knows what he is getting into. They are personal and you know that they aren't rote, pat answers — that the kid is not just giving a canned response to the question."

Panelists do not want to hear such comments as: "I want to go to get a great education." A great education is available at lots of colleges and universities.

Nor do they want to hear: "I want to go because my parents cannot afford to send me to college and this is the way for me to get a free education." The panelists who object strongly to this kind of answer point out that the Academy really is not free; a great amount of work is required to get through four years and, in addition, the graduate has to pay the government back by serving at least five years on active duty.

What panelists are really trying to determine is whether or not you really want to serve in the Army. That is the sole purpose of the Academy's existence; it is there to prepare a select group of Army officers to serve their nation in times of peace and war.

Does that mean that you have to convince the panel that you intend to remain in the military and make it a 20- or 30-year career?

Some panelists would, indeed, like to hear that kind of declaration. But a majority said they were skeptical of 17- and 18-year olds making such statements. Typical was a university professor from Pennsylvania: "He can say, 'I'm thinking about a military career, but I don't know for sure that is what I'll be doing [in the future].' That's okay, but anybody who tells me at eighteen that he knows he's going to be a professional soldier, that's malarkey. He has to be a lot more mature than the kids at the university where I'm teaching because they're never that sure about their future."

★ *What are you going to do if you don't get in?*

The real wording of this questions should be: "How serious are you about wanting an military career?"

If you are, indeed, serious, the panel would expect you to say that while West Point is your first choice, you would accept an appointment to another service academy. They would expect that you have also applied for an ROTC scholarship. Or that you plan on attending a college with an ROTC unit so you can get the military experience and a year's college which will help you when you apply again next year. A West Point graduate who sits on a congressional nomination panel explains, "We're not necessarily looking for a candidate who says the military is the only thing they would do, but we are looking for someone who wants to serve their country, not at what's in it for them."

If you do not have a contingency plan, the panel is likely to think that you have only a shallow desire to go to the Academy. Consequently, do not expect high marks with an answer like, "Oh, I think I'll just go to Ponderosa College and study engineering."

One Air Force cadet said this question helped him overcome a not-so-competitive GPA (he had good SAT scores, sports, and extracurricular activities): "I told them that if they didn't give me a nomination this year, I'd be back every year until I was too old. I think that convinced them how badly I wanted it, and to take a chance on me." It worked.

★ Suppose you went to the Academy and later caught your best friend cheating. Could you turn in your friend?

Some version of this question is asked to see how well you have researched the subject of the Honor Code. The thinking of the panel is that a highly motivated candidate would know about that Honor Code and would already have thought about some of the consequences of living with it. So this question is just another one aimed to measure your motivation. (For a discussion of the Honor Code see Chapter 22.)

★ What makes you think you can stand the stress?

This question is asked so you will talk about yourself. The panel wants to hear about the difficult, stressful situations you have encountered in your lifetime. Perhaps those were on the football field with a tough coach who yelled at you all the time. If so, describe the coach's actions and how you handled the criticism.

But there are other possibilities you might discuss. For example, if your parents are divorced and you suffered in some way in the aftermath, do not be afraid to describe how you coped with the problem.

Basically the panel wants to see if you have had any experience coping with stress. They do not want to hear answers like, "Oh, I'm pretty tough; I can handle it," or "I just know I can do it."

The key to answering this question successfully is to talk freely about yourself and give specific examples that show you have some experience with stressful situations.

★ Who is your hero (or someone you admire)?

This is a favorite question of some panelists so you should be ready for it. But with whomever you mention, you should also be ready to explain why you selected that person.

Of course, your rationale will give the panel more insight into your beliefs and attitudes.

One word of caution. Before going into the interview it would be prudent to check out the political bias of the congressman. A liberal, anti-military congressman may select panelists with that same philosophy. Consequently, they might not think so highly of a choice like Douglas MacArthur or George Patton. On the other hand, a conservative congressman might have the same kind of panel that would grimace at the mention of Jane Fonda (who was a very militant anti-Vietnam activist) or your favorite rap singer whom the panel is not likely to know or appreciate.

★ *How do you think the United States should deal with ISIS?*

Many panels will ask a current events question like the one above. Some panelists believe that academy candidates should be a cut above the average good student and be aware of world events. However, those panelists are probably in the minority.

According to most panelists who were interviewed, current events questions are asked primarily so the panel can see how candidates handle themselves with such a question. In other words, they think that most candidates will not know much about the question that was asked. But, will the candidate fluster or try to bluff his way through an answer? Or will the candidate have the poise and confidence to look the panelists in the eye and say, "I'm sorry, but I can't answer that. I have been so busy the past two weeks I haven't even picked up a newspaper or a news magazine."

It might also help if candidates would explain that they are aware that knowledge of current events is required by plebes at the Academy. But then be prepared for this question: "If you are too busy now to keep up with current events, how are you ever going to do it at the Academy when the pressure is much, much greater?"

★ *What are your strongest and weakest points?*

This is a common question designed, not so the panel can pick at your weaknesses, but to get you to talk about yourself.

Show confidence when you talk about your strongest points. Many panelists say that young people are often too shy when talking about themselves. Try to remember that one of the things the panel is doing is evaluating your potential ability as an Army officer. And a leader cannot be shy. On the contrary such a leader must project a strong image. So do not hesitate with the panel. They asked you to talk about your strengths so this will probably be your best opportunity during the interview to sell yourself.[1]

Be cautious when discussing your weak points. The panel does not want to hear about your sins or mistakes. Mainly they want to know what traits you are working to improve upon. For example, do you procrastinate like most people? If so, admit it, but also explain what you have done recently to try to overcome that weakness. Do you keep a messy room? If so, describe how you are trying to change so you will be ready for the orderliness at the Academy. Do you have a quick temper? This is a more serious weakness, so be ready to

---

[1]One panelist cautioned: "Sell yourself, but use humility. Don't come across as a boastful." Remember, they have seen your record.

Sue Ross

explain how you are learning to control it.

★ *How are you preparing physically?*

The Academy is a very physical place and most panelists know it. Therefore, you should be prepared to discuss a specific physical conditioning program that you plan to follow. If you are familiar with and participating in the Academy's recommended physical preparation plan, even better.

You are not likely to get good marks for an answer like, "Oh, I played football; I'm in good shape."

★ *How have you handled failure?*

It is very difficult for some young people — particularly high achievers who are good candidates — to handle failure. To be sure, some high achievers have never experienced failure.

However, if a panelist asks that question, it is probably because he or she knows that failure at the Academy is inevitable. Not major failure, of course, but failure in small things is purposely induced by the upperclassmen.

So think about this question before you go before a panel. If you have not experienced failure, you should present an attitude that says, "If I fail and I have done my best, then I can't do anything else about it. But the important thing about me is that if you keep knocking me down I will keep getting up. Temporary failures are not important to me. I am not the kind of person who gives up when things are going bad. I am not a quitter."

HOW TO PREPARE

So much for the typical questions. The next thing you should know about the interviews is how to prepare for them.

The most important thing you can do is ARRANGE A PRACTICE INTERVIEW. This may sound silly to some candidates and in fact one Air Force cadet said, when the practice interview was mentioned in a discussion, "What kid is going to go out and arrange something like that?"

The fact is, most candidates discover that they do significantly better in their second interview than they did in their first one. They give better answers to the questions. And they are more poised and

Be prepared to explain why you want to attend West Point.
Senator Al Franken

confident.

Another fact is that you are reading this book because you want to get an edge on your competition. So try to remember what the cadet said and realize that he is right. Most of your competitors will not take the trouble to arrange a practice interview. So do what they will not do and get ahead of them!

Some of the best people to conduct a practice interview are military officers from any branch of the service. They can be located in almost any community or neighborhood and most would be very willing to give you a good workout — especially retired officers who have plenty of free time. Your MALO may also work with you.

We have been telling you that your parents should be hands off in the application process; however, they may be a big help preparing you for the interview process. The congressional interviews are not so different from many job interviews, so your mom or dad — or a family friend — can give you tips and help you practice, even if they have no military experience. Whom you go to for help matters less than making sure you practice before your interview.

As soon as you know when your congressional interviews are to be held, begin making specific plans for them.

For example, plan what you are going to wear well ahead of time so your clothes can be ready. As for what you should wear, most panelists were in agreement.

Most panelists believe that men should wear slacks, a dress shirt and tie. Many suggested that a sport coat should also be worn, however most felt that a candidate should not go out and buy something just for an interview. Several said they would just as soon see a young man in a nice sweater as a coat.

Several panelists mentioned shoes — some with negative comments about old dirty "sneakers" and leather shoes that were scuffed and unshined. The best advice is to wear well shined leather shoes if you have them. Said one panelist, "Wear a suit or a coat and tie. Make your best first impression. Make sure your hair is neat, and wear shoes other than tennis shoes. For women, wear a nice, conservative outfit. Be professional. Treat it like a job interview."

There was mixed advice about female dress, whether or not a dress or skirt is preferable to slacks. Most who commented on the matter did agree female candidates should not come dressed like they were going to a party. Go especially easy on frills, jewelry, makeup and high heels. Said a woman panelist from Nebraska, "I'll never forget one girl who came in teetering on three-inch high heels; the panel was not impressed."

While discussing clothing that candidates should wear, almost every panelist gave examples of bad taste that they could remember, such as color mismatches of ties and socks. So get some help in coordinating colors if you are in doubt about your judgment.

Others mentioned poor grooming — things like dirty fingernails and unwashed or uncombed hair. Several panelists laughed about some candidates who come in jeans, T-shirt, without socks or in a sweat suit. One staffer, laughing and shaking her head, remembered a candidate who came in shorts and sandals.

A retired general and graduate of West Point from Washington State perhaps summed up the matter the best. After discussing his belief that young men should appear in a coat and tie if they can, he said: "[These kids] are looking at a very significant event in their lives. That little session could change the next thirty-five years of their lives. A lot of the kids come in, first of all, not fully appreciating that, and certainly not showing much deference to the critical juncture where they find themselves."

One panelist emphasized that Junior ROTC cadets should wear their uniform. "I've seen many candidates who were involved in JROTC, but only two who came in uniform. For our committee, those who came in uniform made a huge impression." Make sure the uniform is as sharp as possible, with a well-ironed shirt and shined shoes.

The candidate should also plan ahead to make sure to be on time. If transportation looks like it might be a problem, plan ahead. Ask for help from your counselor or your MALO. Said one staffer, "Map the route ahead of time. Read the letter informing you of your interview very carefully. We've had candidates lose their letter, come at the wrong time, even come to our office when we were using a different location for the interviews. Read the letter closely!"

And by all means, telephone the congressional staffer should an emergency arise and you will be late for the interview or miss it altogether. Make sure your reason stands up to scrutiny. As the staffer explained, "We conduct about 125 interviews each year. When someone calls to reschedule for a dumb reason, it makes us wonder about their commitment." They realize you are involved in many activities — all serious candidates are. But if you can't rearrange your schedule to make this important interview, it had better be for a very impressive reason.

PRESENT YOUR BEST SELF

Now the planning is over. You are sitting in the congressman's outer office with many other candidates, waiting. And you are nervous. But you look around and see only one or two who look like you feel. But the others…they look so calm! Seeing these others looking so confident may suddenly cause your self-image to fade. You may even begin doubting whether or not you should be competing in their league. And you may ask yourself: Wouldn't it be better just to ease out of the room and forget about the whole thing?

Not if you really believe you have what it takes to be a leader. You can believe that everyone waiting with you is just as nervous as you are.

Leaders must have the ability to control their fears and make those around them believe that they are full of confidence. And if those who are waiting with you for an interview do, indeed, convince you that they are confident, give them an "A" for leadership potential. They are probably as nervous as you are, only they are controlling it and projecting another image.

So, make up your mind that you, too, are going to take control and project a confident image. That is what the panelists will be looking for. Said a rough-talking, retired colonel from Georgia, "[The interview] is a test. Part of the challenge is to keep from being flustered. You get a guy who goes all to pieces and wets his pants — you don't want him leading a platoon in combat and creating a panic."

What else can you do while you are waiting? Rather than rehearsing possible answers to questions in your mind, you are probably better off trying to keep your mind uncluttered so you can give fresh, thoughtful, original answers to the questions when you get before the panel. Several panelists mentioned candidates who appeared to have all their answers memorized, then gave them with robot-like speeches.

Many panelists also complained about candidates who give brief answers to questions. "To get anything out of some of them, you almost have to drag it out," was a typical comment. While you are waiting, try to remember that the panel is waiting to hear what you are going to say. They want to do very little of the talking. So convince yourself that when they start asking questions you are not just going to give an answer — you are going to discuss the question with them.

Also program your mind so you are ready to discuss yourself. Every question they ask will be of a personal nature to some degree. Project your personality into that discussion.

One further thing you can do while waiting is to ask the receptionist or staffer for a list of the names of the panel. You might not be able to memorize all of them, but you should at least know the name of the chairman. Later, it will be impressive if you can reply to Mr. Williams or Mrs. Johnson when you only heard their names once during the introduction.

Now the time has finally come; it is your turn to go in and meet the panel. Usually the staffer will come out to the waiting area and escort you into the room with the panel. Then you will be introduced, typically to the chairman first; then to the other panelists.

Who will sit on the panel? It varies widely from congressman to congressman. They may be ex-military officers, community leaders, or parents. There may be only two or half a dozen. They all bring their own experiences and values to the interview, as well as guidance from the congressman as to what he or she is looking for in a service academy candidate.

If it seems appropriate and natural, shake hands with the chairman and, perhaps, with the others as well. And if you do that, shake hands with a firm grip. Many people harbor very negative feelings about any person who gives them a limp handshake.

You will be given a chair in front of the panel and it is important that you sit erect. Of course, you will not be expected to sit as erect as you would a year later should you make it into the Academy. But panelists often criticized the posture of candidates, especially those who slumped badly.

Panelists were also critical of those who cannot control their hands. Excessive wringing of the hands was mentioned several times, as was nervous movement. Probably the best advice is to put your hands in your lap or the arms of the chair and use them only for your natural gestures.

Another thing that bothered panelists was the use of current high school slang, and the excessive use of "you knows," "umms" and "likes." Candidates who expressed themselves well and who used good grammar were commended. Panelists also commented favorably about candidates who exhibited good manners and who used respectful terms like "sir" and "ma'am."

Some panelists believe that candidates should maintain eye contact throughout the interview. The strongest statement came from a panelist in Arizona who served on a panel one of us observed. She said, "That's the single, most important thing that you can tell a kid who is going before a panel. Have him make eye contact and keep it. Now I don't mean that he is to look at my hairline or at my chin or at my nose. I want the candidate looking at my eyes! I watch for this with each candidate. The ones who are insecure and lack confidence don't do it — at least that is my impression. Those who have poise and confidence in themselves do. And which do I want to send to a service academy? No way am I going to vote for a kid who doesn't have confidence in himself, because he'll never make it."

You can also demonstrate confidence by hesitating after one of the panelists asks you a question. The natural reaction, if you are tense, is to blurt out answers as fast as possible. Fight that tendency. Pause and think for a few seconds before you reply. Of course, that requires poise on your part. But outward poise is one of the best indicators of inner confidence.

Panelists also have complained that candidates often either do not listen to the questions that are asked or that they ignore them. "Either way, he makes a bad mistake," said a panel chairman. "The candidates who consistently get the highest ratings are those who answer the questions precisely."

How do you give an answer that is not too brief or too rambling? One Admissions Liaison Officer (the Air Force counterpart to the MALO) gives the following tip for formulating your answers: "I like the STAR method — it stands for Situation or Task, Action, and Result." This simple technique keeps the candidate from giving short yes or no answers that do not fully answer the question. For example, if you are asked about your weaknesses or your ability to handle failure, you could describe the Situation or Task you had trouble with, then what Action you took to improve yourself, and the Result of that action. When you do your practice interview, get comfortable with this or a similar technique for answering.

At the end of the interview the candidate is usually asked if he or she has any questions of the panel. Typically, say the panelists, the candidates are surprised and often they think they should ask something. They often ask, "When am I going to know something?" which is a question that is better asked of the staffer before or after the interview.

If you know that one of the panelists is a service academy graduate or veteran, you could ask a question about their service, such as what they liked best about serving in the military. If you do not have a specific question in mind, several panelists suggested that the candidate should use the time offered to say something like: "I really don't have a question, but there are a couple of things you didn't ask me which I think are important for you to consider. Would you mind if I just took a couple of minutes to go over them?"

Remember that panelists are human. In the course of one or two days of interviews they will sometimes forget to ask things that are important. So, during the interview, keep in mind the things you have not been asked — especially those things, when brought out, that might make a difference in your evaluation. Then use the time at the end of the interview to point out those things.

Now the interview is over. The chairman will probably stand up, and perhaps the other panelists, too. If it seems natural, shake hands again. But for sure, thank the panelists for giving you the opportunity to meet with them. Also, make it a point to *thank the staffer, too.*

PRACTICE, PRACTICE, PRACTICE!

This chapter is nearly over and the author can breathe a sigh of relief, having relayed to you every important bit of advice that came from all the panelists and staffers.

But you, the candidate, cannot relax. You still have the interviews to face. And probably you are trying to juggle all the important dos and don'ts in your mind:
- Do use good English
- Do give complete answers, but …
- Don't ramble
- Don't wring your hands
- Don't slump in the chair
- Don't use high school slang or too many "you knows"
- Do look the panelists in the eye
- Do use good manners
- Etc., etc., etc.

All of that together is enough to put anybody's mind into overload, especially when you have to go into a room with strangers for the first time.

And what to do about that? Perhaps the advice in the following story might help.

The original author of this book received a telephone call from a candidate in Kentucky whose father is an old friend. The candidate had used the raw manuscript of an earlier edition of this book to guide his own candidacy. He called with the news that he had just received his appointment. That was wonderful news, of course, and, in the discussion that followed, the young man was asked what advice helped him the most.

"There is no doubt about that," the young man replied. "The recommendation you made to do a practice interview is the best advice in that manuscript. Be sure and put that in the book."

The author replied: "Should I say anything more about the practice interview — something that would persuade others to do it?"

"Yes, tell them that it helped tremendously, and I mean tremendously!"

That conversation relates directly to the problem of the candidate trying to keep all the dos and don'ts in mind as the first interview is impending. And the best advice for the candidate is: Do not let the first interview you do be the one that counts.

Arrange one or more practice interviews. And use them to *practice* the dos and *practice* avoiding the don'ts!

CHAPTER 13

Alternate Routes to West Point

You have submitted all the paperwork required by the Military Academy. You completed your nomination interviews. And now you wait, and wait.

Weeks pass. Then you start getting bad news. You did not receive a nomination from your representative and senators. Or perhaps you got a nomination, but then you got a letter saying that you did not get an appointment.

Now what?

Is your dream of attending the West Point over? Are you sure you will never be a cadet or a graduate of the Academy?

If you are ready to give up already, perhaps the Academy was not for you in the first place. The Academy is not for quitters; it's for those who have the ability to face failure, pick themselves up, and figure out how to succeed the next time.

This chapter is directed at those with that kind of determination. If you fail to get in the first time you apply, ask yourself a few hard questions. Am I really qualified for West Point? If not, can I become qualified in the future? If you can honestly say yes, and you truly want to go to the Academy, don't give up yet!

Here's why: In each entering class, approximately 300 of those appointed do not come in right out of high school. Roughly one third of new plebes enter the Academy by alternate routes. Many of them faced rejection the first time they applied. If you are determined, an alternate route may work for you as well.

So, what should you do next?

If you did not get a nomination, call one or more of the congressional staffers who have your file. Explain that you have no intention of giving up—that you want to apply again next year. Then ask the staffer if he or she would please look over your file and make recommendations on what you can do to make yourself a better candidate. Realize, of course, that the staffer probably cannot do this immediately while you are on the telephone. So, with your request, also ask when it would be convenient for you to call back. This will give the staffer time to review your case and to think of advice that would be most helpful.

If you received a nomination but not an appointment, there are two people you should contact. One is your MALO. The other is your regional admission commander's office (this person may already have made contact with you earlier in the process to give you advice). Try to convince both that you are determined to do whatever you have to do to get accepted for the next class. Then, as with the congressional staffers, give them time to review your application before you call them again. Also, you may receive a letter from the admissions office at several points in the process, providing you feedback on how to become more competitive.

While you are consulting with those who will be discussing your weaknesses or deficiencies, be very careful not to get defensive about yourself. Just listen to what they are telling you, and even if you think they are wrong, thank them for their feedback.
After the consultations, the next step is to evaluate what you have heard. Then you should develop a plan of action based upon your options.

HOW TO BECOME MORE COMPETITIVE

One of the most common problems of unsuccessful candidates is an academic deficiency—demonstrated by a low grade point average or low test scores: SAT, ACT, or a combination of both. If this is your problem, you must demonstrate as soon as possible that you are capable of academic success at the Academy.

How?

Get into a college as soon as you can. And take hard courses. If you prepared for it in high school, take calculus. Take English. And take chemistry. And work as hard as you can. Do more than you are assigned. Get as many A's as you can.

Also, take the SAT and ACT as many times as you can—remember, it is your highest score that counts.

In addition to your college classes you should also consider taking a specialized course designed to help you increase your SAT and ACT scores. Ask your high school or college counselor about local programs. Another option is to check your Yellow Pages under "Tutoring."

What kind of college should you attend?

A general recommendation would be to go to the best college you can afford and the best college that will admit you. Even better would be a college that has an ROTC (Reserve Officer Training Corps) unit that will accept you.

Ideally you should try to get into an Army ROTC program. However, if this is not possible, do not hesitate to get into a Navy or Air Force unit—you are seeking an opportunity to prove yourself to military officers. The branch of service is of minor importance.

Perhaps your problem is not an academic deficiency. Perhaps you were not involved in many extracurricular activities while in high school. Perhaps those who evaluated your application felt that you were too single-focused on academics to make a good cadet. If so, what can you do?

First, go on to college and do what has already been recommended. But get active in things other than academics. If you are in ROTC, get active and try to become a leader in whatever other clubs the unit sponsors that interests you. As one admissions officer at West Point said, "Get in and get dirty...and prove yourself."

ROTC cadets and midshipmen can compete for a special category of nomination. But even more important, being successful in ROTC will demonstrate your commitment to becoming an officer, and your ability to handle military and academic challenges at the same time.

Get involved in student government, the school newspaper, dramatics, intramural sports, clubs, or whatever else interests you. And strive for leadership positions.

Do not worry that you cannot be elected president of a club as a freshman. Do what you can. Volunteer for committees and take as much responsibility as the organization will give you. There are always opportunities. For example, few organizations will deny an eager freshman the opportunity to lead a clean-up committee.

And remember what you are seeking. You are seeking leadership experience. Also you are seeking leadership credentials that you can cite on your next application.

One more thing to remember: As you are transitioning from high school to college life with all its challenges, your nomination and admissions paperwork will be coming due again. That means you have a lot to do, but it also means you will impress people with your determination and ability to handle both at once.

JOIN THE FORCE

What if you cannot afford college? You can enlist in the Army—the active force, or the Guard or Reserve—with the goal of earning one of the appointments given enlisted members each year.

You should realize that this option is much more risky than the college option. With the college option you can go on and get your degree, then perhaps get an officer's commission. But if you enlist, you might never get to be an officer. You might join for three or four years, not be admitted to the Academy, and end your enlistment without any college credit.

If you do decide to join the Army, here is some advice that has been handed down from others who have entered the Academy from that route.

First, you must excel at everything you do in order to earn good recommendations from your supervising officers. In boot camp, try to be the outstanding trainee. In whatever technical training program you enter after that, strive to be at the top of your class both in academics and in military qualities. Later, when you are given your active-duty assignment, try to be the best Soldier you know how to be.

In addition, make sure you have a copy of the regulation that explains the academy application procedure. It is not uncommon for personnel to know very little about the procedure. So do not depend upon someone else to tell you how to apply.

Let your supervising non-commissioned officers (NCOs) and officers know that your goal is to attend the Academy. Those supervisors may give you responsibilities that will allow you to prove that you have leadership potential.

A word of caution: Some of your peers or immediate supervisors may not understand why you want to go to the Academy. They may even try to talk you out of pursuing an appointment. Why? They may feel you are betraying the enlisted force by seeking an officer's commission. They may resent you for taking a valuable asset (you: a hard-working, well-trained young troop) away from the unit. Or they may be officers who were commissioned through ROTC or OCS who do not like West Pointers in general for one reason or another.

Said one plebe who had been enlisted, "My commander tried to talk me out of it. I got thrashed by my NCOs—they didn't want to lose a soldier. I had to do lots of pushups!" You will have to resolve to stay committed to your goals, and look past this kind of short-sightedness to pursue them. Said another, "Enlist. You will come in with a better perspective on why you're here. It makes everything here easier. You can say, "I've been there [in the Army]."

While you work through the process, remember that you still have opportunities to improve your academic ability. Enlisted personnel can subscribe to a number of college-level correspondence courses. Also, most bases have off-duty college classes available that you may be able to take.

Few go directly from the Army into the Academy. Most spend a year at the U.S. Military Academy Preparatory School, which is collocated with the Military Academy on the grounds of West Point. The purpose of USMAPS is to bring potential cadets "up to speed" in math, English, science, and information technology. Military and athletic training is also included, which will give you a head start on juggling all that is required during your plebe year.

PREP SCHOOLS

Prep schools are designed for promising candidates who are not quite ready to enter an academy. Often these are candidates who have demonstrated leadership potential, but who are slightly deficient academically. Many are recruited athletes or enlisted personnel.

You cannot apply directly to USMAPS. Your application to the Academy serves that purpose. The admission board will offer Prep School appointments to certain promising candidates who do not get appointments.

Candidates typically react in one of two ways when they are offered the prep school option. One candidate says, "Wow, that's a great opportunity. Where do I sign?"

The other candidate says, "What! You expect me to waste a year of my life in a prep school? You have to be kidding. I would rather forget about the whole thing and just go on to a college and take ROTC."

Before you react either way, you should think about some of the advantages of the Prep School option. First, it will give you a chance to strengthen your background in the subjects that are most difficult for first-year cadets. More than one graduate emphasized that the Prep School will lessen the academic shock you feel plebe year.

Second, and perhaps more important, the instructors will see to it that you learn how to study. Not knowing how to study is the biggest problem of first-year midshipmen who enter an academy right out of high school.

Third, you will have one more year of maturity before you start the rigorous schedule of a plebe. That year of maturity will help you adapt to the many stresses of that first year. You will also be over the pain of homesickness, a malaise that creates problems for many who leave home for the first time.

Fourth, you will learn a great deal about military training. You will know how to shine your shoes and put your room in inspection order, and you will learn some of the military knowledge and culture that most plebes first encounter on Induction Day. This knowledge will give you more time to focus on your studies, and the opportunity to establish yourself as a leader among your Academy classmates. Every cadet interviewed who had gone to USMAPS said the year spent at Prep School made the military demands of plebe year much easier.

Said one plebe, "Prep School gave me things I'd never thought about, It set me up for success. If gives you a year to open your eyes, a year to be away from home and be on your own. It's a good middle step. [If you are offered a Prep School appointment, it's because] they see your potential, but see a deficiency or they wouldn't put you there. I would do it again." For more information about the Prep School, see usma.edu/USMAPS.

Nearly everyone who attends prep school says it was a great opportunity to mature and be more prepared for the Academy.   *United States Military Academy*

USMAPS is not the only prep school option you may be offered. Through the West Point Association of Graduations, the West Point Preparatory Scholarship Program offers scholarships to competitive candidates to attend other prep schools or colleges. There are two ways candidates can be offered one of these scholarships. The first is to be recommended by the West Point admissions office. The second is to apply directly. Either way, you must have completed your full application to West Point. Over 85 percent of WPPSP recipients get an appointment after completing prep school. For more information, visit **www.westpointaog.org**.

Whether at USMAPS or another prep school, the year will be very well spent.

HOW TO SURVIVE

CHAPTER 14
The Challenging Plebe Year

Your West Point experience officially begins when you report in the to the cadet in the red sash — an upperclassmen who will welcome you in a way that lets you know a) expectations are very high at the Academy, and b) you are already falling short of those expectations. From that moment, you will have no doubt that your days as high school superstar are over.

That feeling of being unable to live up to the high expectations of the upperclassmen will dominate your experience as a new cadet in Cadet Basic Training, and continue through much, if not all, of your plebe year. There will be days when you wonder if it will ever end.

The first step to surviving this long and demanding year is knowing what to expect and understanding why you are being treated this way.

A DAY IN THE LIFE OF A PLEBE

During CBT, no two days will be alike. But they will begin with an early (around 5:00) wakeup, breakfast, marching, and Physical Training — PT. Activities will include combat related training such as marksmanship, obstacle courses, and road marches. You will spend several nights in the field, sleeping in a tent. You will also take care of many administrative tasks — taking placement tests for the academic year, listening to briefings, filling out paperwork, getting uniforms and other issue items.

You will be learning more information in less time than you ever thought possible. You will learn how to wear your uniform, how to put your room in inspection order, how to march and salute, and seemingly endless facts about the Army and West Point — plebe knowledge.

One plebe remembers CBT like this, "Your job as a new cadet is simple. You

Every thing plebes do will be critiqued, even how they eat.

United States Military Academy

stand around a lot, learn knowledge, do simple tasks. You don't have to think very much. But it's still stressful. You never know what is going to happen next."

Said another, It's only seven weeks, and it goes by fast. But it's a huge culture shock. They even tell you how to eat. It makes you crazy."

Once the academic year begins, your days will settle into a routine. Sometime around 6:00 a.m., you will get up and get dressed and perform your duties such as delivering papers or handing out laundry. You may be tasked to call minutes, which requires plebes to yell out the amount of time left until the next formation — mainly an opportunity to make a mistake and be criticized for it.

You must leave your room in inspection order and report to the morning formation in a perfect uniform, because your squad leader will inspect and critique your appearance. You will also be quizzed on the menus for the day's meals, current events, and plebe knowledge. If you make a mistake, your punishment will probably be an assignment to learn extra knowledge — something you really do not need!

You can only speak when spoken to, and must answer questions with one of four responses, "Yes, sir (or ma'am, as appropriate)," "No, sir," "Sir I do not understand," and "No excuse, sir."

At 7:30, classes begin. Some classes meet for one hour and some for two. Most classes meet every other day. While the day is focused on being a student, you can never forget you are a plebe. You must walk at attention, square your corners, stay to the right in all hallways, and refrain from talking.

After class, if you are not an intercollegiate athlete, you will play intramural sports every other day. The other days, afternoons will be spent on drill, group runs, orienteering, or other military training. Before dinner, you will perform more duties. Then, at

Being accepted into the Corps of Cadets after CBT is a big accomplishment. *United States Military Academy*

last, you are "free" to do your homework and studying. One group of plebes said that most of them stay up until about 12:00 or 1:00 trying to get everything done.

Now you know a bit about what the plebe year is like. But why? What is the purpose of all the rules and criticism?"

YOU'RE IN THE ARMY NOW

When you report for CBT as a wide-eyed civilian teenager, you have just four short years to become an officer who can lead other soldiers — some much older and more experienced. The amount of information you must learn in those four years is overwhelming. You must also practice warfighting skills and become physically as strong as possible.

But beyond that, you must become a part of the Army. You must understand the culture and traditions and way of life so completely that being a soldier is second nature. The director of military instruction explains that the military training is designed to do two things: "Bring new cadets into the culture of the Army and the Corps [of Cadets], and make them proficient as soldiers."

Sometimes, it will seem like harassment with no real purpose. But you are being taught to follow orders, pay attention to details, and deal with stress so you will be an effective Army officer.

Explained a firstclass cadet, "Your uniform has to look right. You are going to pay attention to detail and you're not going to make little mistakes at table duties. All the little things, tucking in your shirt, crooked tie or tie straight, laying on your jacket, announcing word for word all this knowledge and history, it's about teaching these kids how to learn a format, how to react under pressure, and pay attention to detail so that the little things become second nature to you, so that when you're a tank commander and you're in the middle of a fight in the middle of the desert, all the little things that go into leading that tank and giving command and operating with the rest of the platoon in the company...that has to be second nature." Soon enough, it will be.

This transformation is so complete that you will already be a new person by the time CBT is over. If your parents are able to visit you at the end of the summer, they will be stunned to find that you have changed so much they barely recognize their son or daughter. You will stand up straighter and talk more confidently. You will probably be more intense and more serious than they remember.

You may not realize how much you have changed until the first time you get to visit home, perhaps at Thanksgiving. You will get together with your closest high school friends, and suddenly find that your lives are so different you feel you are from another planet.

FOLLOW THE LEADER

West Point is supposed to prepare you to be a leader. How does being criticized and stressed constantly prepare you to lead? In the words of a plebe who had been an enlisted soldier before coming to West Point, "To lead, you first have to follow."

One of the basic principles of leadership at the Academy is that you cannot be a good leader unless you have viewed leadership from the receiving end. There is no better way to study what motivates people than to watch someone try to motivate you. You will have a full year of intense leadership study from this perspective.

Will all the leadership lessons be positive? Probably not. Remember that the upperclassmen are learning how to be leaders by "practicing" on the plebes. Rest assured that they will make mistakes. There will be upperclass cadets whom you want to emulate. On the other hand, some upperclass cadets will use methods that do not work. Cadets and graduates who have been through this experience will tell you to remember both the good and bad lessons as you figure out what kind of leader you want to be.

A plebe explained it this way: "The whole place is a leadership lab. [The upperclass] are trying to figure it out too, especially the cows [sophomore cadets]. You might get someone who doesn't know how to lead. You can learn from that too. I keep a leadership journal and take notes on the leadership I see — the things that are right or wrong."

GET TO KNOW FAILURE

You probably do not think of yourself as a failure, or you would not be a serious contender for an appointment to West Point. That will change if you go to the Academy. Plebes— every single one of them, without exception — will get a personal introduction to failure. Everyone who has been to West Point will agree.

Said a colonel, "Even if you were in the top 10 percent of your high school, you may not even be in the top half of your class at the Academy. You are now a little fish. The rules are rigged. You simply can't be right all the time. You are set up for failure so you learn how to deal with it. You will learn to set priorities and accept the consequences."

And a first classman: "You're going to fail. You have to fail to get better. No matter how good you are. Even the first captain [the highest-ranking cadet in the Corps]. I know him. Great guy. He makes mistakes and made mistakes. But, it's because he learned from them that he's as an amazing a guy as he is now."

And a plebe: "I thought they would leave me alone if I did a good job and was trying as hard as I could. Wrong! They get on you know matter what. You can't escape the criticism. That was the hardest thing for me, knowing no matter how well I did, I was still going to get chewed on." Another plebe put it more succinctly: "Everyone fails. Get used to it."

While all plebes get criticized, they all want to avoid being "That Guy." That Guy is the plebe who always seems to be in the wrong place, doing the wrong thing, messing up. He is also known as a "spaz" or a "tie-up." He becomes the butt of jokes and the target of constant criticism.

But even if you are not That Guy, you will be given more tasks that you can complete, and held to a higher standard than you can possibly meet. We guarantee it. Why are they so determined to see you fail?

One reason is to make you humble. The Army does not need the smug and self-assured high school superstar. A cocky or arrogant soldier will not be a good leader. Good leaders understand the frustrations and failings of their subordinates. Good leaders know their own weaknesses and strengths.

The second is to teach you how to accept criticism. You must be determined to improve and learn every day, and push yourself to keep getting better. You must also learn to accept responsibility for your shortcomings without excuses, even when you did your best — that is why one of the plebe responses is, "No excuse, sir."

FIND NEW LIMITS

The plebe year also designed to destroy your old conception of how much you can accomplish. One officer explained, "We teach cadets to live with the bad decisions they make under enormous stress and on too little sleep. And we teach you how far you can go." In the face of constant criticism, you will work harder, focus more, and achieve more than you ever thought possible.

You will explore your physical limits and your mental limits. If you fail to meet standards in memorizing plebe knowledge, you will be assigned even more knowledge. The only way to stop that evil cycle is to get on top of it. If you fail to meet physical standards, you will be assigned extra physical conditioning until you pass.

You will also have an opportunity every single day to wake up and recommit yourself — find your emotional limits. The Director of Military Instruction, a colonel, explains, "We make them uncomfortable on purpose, to examine who they are and what they stand for. A monkey can do pushups. It's the emotional coping that's hard."

Said a first classman about to graduate, "I know myself. I know myself way better than I did when I came out of high school. I know my limitations and I know that I can always exceed my limitations if I just believe in myself. Confidence. As confident as I was coming out of high school, I'm a thousand times more confident now. At the same time, with all that confidence I have in myself, I'm also more humble because of what I'm doing. Know that you're going to serve the nation, as cliché as it may sound, is a very humbling experience."

The major in charge of military training explained it this way: "Remember it's a means to an end, your ticket to becoming part of the Corps of Cadets and all West Point has to offer. Learn to be a team player, do what you have to do with a positive attitude. It takes grit and humility. You may have a day when you are down and frustrated, and you may feel like a failure. But true failure is quitting. Keep going. Don't lose sight of your end goal." Plebe year will be hard, no matter who you are or how good you are. But remember, thousands and thousands of plebes before you have survived the challenging first year at West Point. Keeping that in mind should help.

CHAPTER 15
Advice from Plebes

Most of the interviews for this chapter were conducted in the mid to late spring semester, so the plebes we talked to had survived at least three quarters of the challenging first year. They had been home on vacation for the holidays, had the opportunity to relax and reflect on their experience so far…and made the decision to come back for more!

Here is their advice.

KEEP THINGS IN PERSPECTIVE

We have already mentioned how important the right frame of mind is at West Point. Attitude was mentioned by many plebes as a critical survival factor.

When you are feeling overwhelmed by hundreds of small tasks that seem to keep coming at you, you tend to lose perspective. The homework is stacking up, the upperclassmen are on your case, and there seems to be no end in sight. You may forget why you ever thought about coming to West Point in the first place.

One of the facts that all plebes must memorize and recite on demand is the number of days until graduation for each class. When you have more than a thousand days until graduation, it feels like an eternity every time you repeat that large number.

The plebes say you must learn to take things one step at a time. During CBT, think about getting through the day, or just to the next meal. Don't think about the entire seven weeks or even the whole week. One plebe advised, "Set small goals — look forward to the first call home, then the end of CBT, then Thanksgiving. Don't focus on the days, like 1197 days left."

Take it a day at a time, but also remember the long view. Remember your goals. You decided to come to West Point to serve your country and become an Army officer. You want to complete all four years successfully and become a part of the Long Gray Line. Said one plebe, "Knowing you're serving for a bigger purpose gets you through." Another agreed, "You tend to look at the 300 meter target, and not what life is going to be like 30 years later." Remember that your West Point degree will serve you well for your entire life. So a few (or even more than a few) bad days as a plebe are worth enduring.

Some of the things you are required to do will not make sense, at least not at first. Plebes advise you to trust the system. One plebe, who had prior enlisted time, explained, "West Point is not the Army. Don't try to make it the Army. West Point is its own institution and has its own traditions. Accept that or you will be miserable." But in the end, "Remember, there is a point to it all." Resist the temptation to question or complain at every turn, which will only serve to frustrate you. Said another, "Embrace the system. Do what you're supposed to do. Sometime down the road you'll understand. You will do a lot that seems stupid. But work together and get through it."

At the same time, do not take it personally if the upper classmen criticize you. One plebe put it this way: "Play the game. Don't let them get to you. If you take it too seriously, it will be a miserable time."

DON'T FORGET TO SLEEP

We already mentioned that time management is a serious challenge at West Point. One easy place to find extra hours is in the middle of the night, and many cadets are tempted to stay up until the early morning hours trying to get everything done. They convince themselves that they can get by on just a few hours of sleep a night.

The problem with this strategy is that when you are tired, you will not be as alert or productive during the day. That means you won't learn as much in class, and you won't get as much homework done during your free periods… which means you will have to stay up later to compensate. It can be a vicious and destructive cycle.

One plebe explained, "I get between two and three hours [sleep] a night. But the way I manage it is I take frequent 20 to 40 minute naps during the day. If I have an hour free, I'll do all my duties and the things I need to do in the first 20 minutes and the last 40 minutes I'll sleep for 20 to 30 minutes of that time." Most cadets cannot succeed with this approach.

Sleeping in class is not only a waste of time, at the Academy it is not permitted. If you feel sleepy, you are expected to stand up so you stay awake. Said the sleep-deprived plebe, "You stand at parade rest. I've had friends pass out standing up in class."

Most plebes figure out that a good night's sleep will help tremendously with time management the next day, so they give themselves a deadline, usually around midnight. After that, no matter what tasks remain, they get some sleep.

Explained one plebe, "I go to bed at taps every night regardless of where I am in my work. Sleep is just as important as homework. It would be better to be in class paying attention and listening having not done the reading than to be in class fighting sleep having done the reading. If you're awake, you'll ingest the information better than if it were one o'clock in the morning and you were half asleep."

One plebe who was averaging four hours of sleep a night discovered he was wasting a lot of time during the day. So he decided to go to bed at 10:30 every night. "I'm doing a lot better. When you get your sleep, you can pay better attention in class. And that makes the homework easier."

Said another, "The first week [of academics] I stayed up until 3 or 4 a.m. every night doing homework. But they want you to pick and choose." In other words, decide what is most important, do that, then go to bed.

SEEK SUPPORT

Although you may not believe it at the time, your plebe year and your classmates will help you create happy memories that you will reflect on for years to come. Close relationships and fun times you have as a plebe will punctuate the challenges and frustrations. Take advantage of your friends whenever you are feeling down or need to de-stress.

"Everyone thinks about quitting," said a plebe. "Most people here had a full ride somewhere else. You can't help but think about it [life at a civilian college]. Find people who motivate you to keep you going. I call my dad or a friend back home."

Advised another plebe, "Depend on your friends. It's easy to stay in your room and feel sorry for yourself. Even ordering a pizza and watching a movie with your company mates can make it better."

Even though you will be very busy as a plebe, West Point will offer you many diversions and distractions, no matter what your interests. One plebe explained, "There are so many clubs you can join. I'm in the fly fishing club. Getting out and fishing relaxes me. There are little things to break the monotony." A change of scenery, and the chance to do something you enjoy and are good at, can be all you need to help you face another week with a positive attitude.

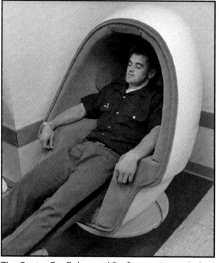

Finding a way to laugh is a necessary antidote to the pressures of the plebe year. Cadets are known for their ingenious sense of humor. One plebe described how his squad got together and played a joke on the upper classmen at the dinner table, politely and properly asking him to pass every single item on the table. Dinner on Thursdays is another time to let loose, when cadets dress up in crazy costumes and

The Center For Enhanced Performance can help you with study and mental skills.

United States Military Academy

get in the mood for the coming weekend's football game or free time. Finding opportunities to laugh and joke will prevent you from taking the pressure, or yourself, too seriously.

SUPPORT SYSTEMS

The Academy also offers more formal support systems for plebes and all cadets. Even if you are feeling that your schedule is already overflowing, taking advantage of these support systems can improve your well-being and help you cope with the stresses of cadet life.

One important support system is the sponsor program. During CBT, you will be matched with a local sponsor family. They may be the family of an officer who works at West Point, a West Point graduate, or just a local family who wants to support cadets. Sponsors provide cadets with a home away from home. Cadets will visit their sponsors to share a meal, play with the sponsors' kids, watch TV, get a change of scenery, and just relax for awhile.

Some cadets don't find a good fit with their assigned sponsors, and end up being "adopted" by someone else — perhaps a professor they like, a coach, or the sponsor of one of their friends. Quite often, the sponsor relationship lasts long after the cadet graduates.

The Cadet Chapel, begun in 1911, is a beautiful and historic place of worship that provides refuge to many cadets. There is also a Catholic Chapel and a Jewish chapel. West Point has chaplains from many different faiths who provide spiritual guidance and counseling. The chapels offers weekend services, fellowship groups, choir programs, and many other special events. Many cadets say that tending to their spiritual beliefs is important to their survival and success. From the start, chaplains and chaplain candidates spend time with new cadets during CPT, allowing relationships to develop and casual conversations to happen. (Chaplains have the highest level of confidentiality.)

The Center for Personal Development — the counseling center — can help you build your coping skills when you are feeling overwhelmed. Staffed by four clinical psychologists, the Center helps cadets deal with the stresses of cadet life as well as many "normal college age issues" such as homesickness, boyfriend or girlfriend problems, and general adjustment. According to one psychologist, cadets are often reluctant to ask for help when they need it: "Even star performers feel stress, but they want to deal

Chaplains and religious activities are a source of support on the dark days. *United States Military Academy*

with it themselves. There is resistance to reaching out for help. You have to recognize that everyone here wants you to succeed. It's not a sign of weakness but a sign of strength to ask for help."

Much of the plebe advice we heard centers on time management and academic success. You will find that advice in Chapter 16. The next chapter contains survival advice from those who have witnessed the plebe year from two different perspectives: that of a plebe going through it, and that of an upperclassman leading and mentoring the plebes.

CHAPTER 16

The Upperclassmen Tell How to Survive

The upperclassmen have the advantage of learning from their own mistakes, and watching those who came after them make similar mistakes. Their advice begins with the ever-present subject of time management.

MAKE EVERY MINUTE COUNT

The most frequently offered advice from the upperclassmen reflects how well they have learned to use all the time in each day. The small windows of time between classes or duties, when added together and used wisely, make a big difference. One cadet summed it up precisely: "Time is precious. Don't waste it." What does that mean to a plebe?

Said one, "Use your free periods. For example, chemistry doesn't always use the whole two hours. So use the extra time to go see your teacher or do some homework." Another agreed, "Use your free hours so you don't have to do everything at night." And another, "Many cadets waste their off hours, but since you're already in the academic mode, it's a really good time to get stuff done."

You will learn how to make use of every minute of your day.

United States Military Academy

Second to using free periods effectively, the next most important time management skill is the ability to prioritize. You will not have time to do everything you are supposed to do. Said one upperclassman, "It's all about priorities. You're not going to get everything done. Figure out what's important and what can get done later." Added another, "No single aspect of the Academy is that hard. It's everything combined. Trying to balance all those things is a wakeup call." The sooner you learn to prioritize tasks and assignments, the more efficiently you will use your time.

As one upperclassman explained, "You have to realize how to prioritize. You divide things into what has to, should, or doesn't need to get done. You have to develop your own system, adapt to your own needs. You'll get homework from all your teachers, and work from the cadet chain of command. You have to figure out what's most important to you." Many of them warned about the dangerous trap of procrastination. Letting yourself fall behind is very risky, because it will be really hard to find time to catch up. Better to look ahead and even work ahead so you never get behind.

BUT TAKE TIME TO RELAX

You may be starting to think all cadets are superhuman, and you, a mere mortal, could never keep up their pace. Don't worry, cadets are human too. They have learned how to carve out small periods of time to decompress. Explained one, "It's tempting to go full speed all day. You have to take a few minutes for yourself—maybe reading or talking to a friend. You need to find an outlet to relieve stress. It helps you focus. You can't go non-stop."

This advice about getting through the "Gloom Period" (the winter months at the beginning of the second semester) came from a first classman: "It's cold. There's snow and ice everywhere. If you're a plebe, you've got no passes. You can't go anywhere. You can't do anything and you're just stuck here. You're wearing a gray uniform. The walls are gray, the sky is gray, and it's easy to get down."

Another agreed that finding an outlet is very important. "Get involved. Do something you like to do. You'll get a whole new body of friends and experiences. Find something."

One suggested, "Find something to look forward to. For me, it was chaplain's time on Wednesday, and getting to sleep in on Sundays." Another added, "I always did no-homework Thursdays, and just hung out with friends." And another: "Don't take it all seriously or you'll hate life." For more information on having fun at West Point, see Chapter 21.

Over and over again, cadets also emphasized the importance of getting adequate sleep. That doesn't mean you can sleep as much as you want, as you may have done on weekends in high school. It does mean that you can't simply stay up until everything is done, or you will become ineffective. You won't do a good job on your homework, and you won't be able to pay attention in class the next day.

BECOMING PART OF SOMETHING BIG

When the plebes talk about keeping perspective, they tend to focus on surviving day to day and remembering that eventually, it will end. The upperclassmen, on the other had, tend to have a different kind of perspective.

The upperclass have already formed an extremely close bond with their classmates, an appreciation of the legacy they are joining, and a respect for the obligation they are about to take on. That perspective helps them persevere.

When asked if he ever thought of quitting, one upperclassman offered, "There's a difference between hating life and seriously considering leaving. I'm not always happy to be here, but I'll always be happy to be from here." Added another, "We have a purpose. We're working toward a long-term goal. We know we're going to be responsible for 30-40 people [after graduation]. We're working toward something greater than ourselves. It feels good to accomplish something knowing that a lot of people couldn't do it or wouldn't want to."

That sense of pride can overcome many stressful days. Remember that you are now part of something special. "West Point attracts a different kind of person, a high quality person, people who voluntarily took on a big challenge. Hard times forge great friendships. There is a commonality that comes from enduring tough times. I'm different from my friends from high school." Appreciate the opportunity to spend your days around such people. Another cadet advised, "Be thankful every day that you are here. You can become desensitized to how special this place is, especially during your plebe year."

The upperclassmen also encourage you to rely on the great friendships formed at West Point whenever you are feeling down or questioning why you came. One recommended, "Don't call your friends at civilian schools. It makes you not want to be here. Depend on your friends [at West Point]. Someone will remind you why you came here."

CHAPTER 17

Academic Survival Tips

You read about the phenomenon we call "Academic Shock" in Chapter 5. Academic Shock is very real. A plebe shared this story: "I think the wake-up is when the people who didn't have to work in high school like myself get that F on their first paper. Out of 17 people in my history class, 11 people got F's on their first paper. I'll bet none of them ever got a D in high school on a paper. So, once you get that first F back on a paper, you realize that this place isn't quite high school."

Not everyone struggles to this degree. Another cadet, whose experiences are probably more typical, said, "I was a straight A student all through high school. Here, I have a 2.9 GPA." But every cadet, as they figure out how to manage the academic load along with the other demands of the Academy, learns through trial and error the methods and techniques that work for them. In this chapter, they share those methods and techniques with you.

TIME MANAGEMENT

Yes, we really are going to talk about time management again, this time with regard to studying and preparing for class. Because if you are not operating at peak efficiency in terms of how you use your study time, you will soon find yourself struggling. One piece of advice we heard repeated often was not to let yourself fall behind.

A thirdclass cadet explained, "The biggest thing about plebe year was staying ahead academically. A lot of times you'll find yourself falling behind. Once you get behind in one area, you're going to start falling behind in others. If you're spending all your time working on homework, you're going to slack off physically. If you're slacking off physically, then you're probably going to be slacking off on things like appearance and what not. That will just draw more heat and more upperclassmen will be trying to take up more of your time. So, I found the best thing to do was to backwards plan."

What, exactly, is backwards planning? "You start from when something is due and then you give yourself increments of time in a reverse fashion. Say it takes two days to research a paper. You subtract two days from that and two days to write your first draft. So you subtract two days from that and once you've gone through the whole process of everything you have to do in order to complete a project, you should get an idea of when you want to start it. I also include in there a buffer should something go wrong. The big thing for me was learning during plebe year not to wait to the last minute to do everything. A lot of times I found myself falling into that trap. If you use your time wisely — it's a hard lesson to learn.

"Right now, as a yearling, I'm really being socked by math and physics so I take time on Fridays and on Sunday morning and Sunday afternoons to work ahead for the week and identify any trouble spots that I may have for those two classes. When it comes time to do any study during the week, then I have ample free time to explore the things that are giving me problems—things I can identify in class. I now get to bed earlier. I'm more alert for class. The big thing though is just to get ahead and stay ahead. Once you do that, everything works out."

A plebe offered similar advice about planning: "I found that it's really beneficial to plan by the week instead of by the day. It really frees up your time. I use the two nights on the weekend to really knock out my homework for the week. All the reading assignments and all the stuff you can get done on your own without any classes. You know that flat out and then the stuff that you do need to get in the classes like math—I usually leave math to do by the day because that really depends upon what you learn in class. As far as English and as far as history and the subjects based on reading, it really helps to knock that stuff out on the weekends. Then you can concentrate on the tougher subjects during the week. That really frees up time for other things: shining shoes, getting your uniform looking good, physical training, etc. Planning by the week instead of by the day will really help you out."

Many plebes are tempted to relax for the entire weekend. Isn't that what weekends are for? Upperclass cadets usually advise that you use a part of the weekend to get ahead. Said one, "Take time to study or you'll fall behind. Use the weekends to your advantage. Don't just watch six movies in a row."

Cadets agree you cannot let yourself fall behind. That means doing the homework and the reading when it is assigned. But more than that, it means making sure you understand everything you should have learned up to that point. If not, fix it by getting help immediately.

A plebe shared this success story of how he turned failing grades around: "What I had to do was do my homework right after class. You go over what you just had to make sure you understand that. If you don't, you go to your instructor for AI [Additional Instruction]. Once you know what you're doing, then you start on the next assignment. That way, if the next class is two days later, you've got time to get help with what you don't understand. You can go to the instructor. You can't do that if you wait till the night before."

Other cadets have figured out that they are more focused at certain times, and use that to become more efficient. "First, I have been using my weekends to get all my work done for Monday and Tuesday and, if possible, Wednesday. That way, at night, I can study the important stuff, things that we're going to be tested on. Another thing I'd recommend: Don't spend time during the day or early evening taking care of the military stuff, like shining your shoes or taking care of your uniform. Save that till the last thing before you go to bed, when your brain is tired. It doesn't take any brain power to polish shoes or polish brass. You can just sit there for 15 or 20 minutes doing that stuff without being totally awake or thinking."

AVOID GETTING LOST IN CYPERSPACE

When you are feeling cut off from the "Real World," tired and stressed, the laptop on your desk offers many connections and distractions. Facebook, YouTube, e-mail, instant messaging, online gaming…the entire internet is waiting for you. It can connect you with your friends from high school, and it doesn't care that you are a lowly plebe.

One cyberthreat you cannot avoid, and therefore must learn to manage, is e-mail. Many cadets report receiving more than a hundred emails per day. Of these, only a small percentage requires attention and action. Cadets advise, "Learn to skim and find the important things. Learn what's important, and keep your inbox clean." They disagree on how frequently you ought to check your email. Regulations require you check it every day, but most cadets agreed that once a day is insufficient to catch all the important messages, such as a new military duty, details on an assignment or a change in classrooms. One upperclassman suggested, "Check it once an hour. Just take a quick break from studying." Some suggest turning the audible alert off so that you are not distracted.

What about the other cyberthreats? Surf with caution. Many cadets tell tales of classmates who got lost in the digital world, and by the time they reappeared, they were so far behind they could not catch up. Said one cadet, "I've seen people fail out because of gaming. You're not supposed to as plebes, but some do. I've seen people resign because their grades got so low." Another cadet offered, "I know someone who switched his entire sleep cycle to play World of Warcraft, someone who got kicked out the summer before his firstclass year. Some people can set rules, assign themselves limited amount of time." Instant messaging, Facebook, and YouTube are also big distractions. Many cadets turn off AIM, or turn off the instant chat on Facebook. Some close down their Facebook accounts entirely, so they are not tempted. The point to remember is that your time is too limited to allow large chunks of it to disappear before you realize it.

A third classman explained, "It's self-discipline. When it comes down to it, you are responsible for your own actions. You have to decide that there are more important things to do with your time."

WHERE TO STUDY

Academic success requires knowing when to study and how much to study. Success also requires learning where to study. The right answer often varies from one cadet to the next, but many agree that their room in the barracks is not the ideal location.

A first classman explained, "The natural tendency is for [plebes] to stay in their room in the evening. They feel safe there, but lots of times it may not be the best study environment. You may have a roommate who is really popular and people like to visit. You can't study because his friends are always coming in and hanging out. Or, maybe your room is really cramped and your roommate is making noise. Lots of things can cause problems. Anyhow, the smart thing for a plebe to do is to go to an academic building or the library to study. You go there, you sit down, you're in an academic setting — you just work better. You perform better. You're kind of in the mindset, 'I'm in class now.' You'll work harder and more efficiently. That's really true. I've done it and I've seen it. I've watched the kids who have like the best grades. You don't see them study in their rooms all the time. They're not around. When it's time to study, they'll go somewhere where they can get their work done."

Another upperclassman agreed: "I can't study in my room. I get along with my roommates too well. Then there's the computer, the phone, people coming in and out. I study in the library or in academic buildings that are open after class. Also, each company has a study room."

Some cadets complained that the library, which is brand new and state of the art, is too attractive for plebes. "The library is a plebe hangout." Another countered, "It depends on where you go. Find a quiet corner. Later at night it gets better, and the higher up you go [the quieter it is]."

Find a place to study that works for you, one free of distractions. The library works well for many cadets. *United States Military Academy*

The right place to study depends on you — how easily distracted you are, and how you work best. Be honest about what you need to study efficiently and effectively. If it means putting on a uniform and going out into the cold to find someplace quiet, do it.

THE CENTER FOR ENHANCED PERFORMANCE

Cadets recommend you take advantage of another valuable resource available to you: The Center for Enhanced Performance. This section would belong equally well in the chapter for intercollegiate athletes, or in the chapter of physical preparedness, or just about any chapter in the book. But many cadets think of academic performance first when they think of this center.

What do they do? Their mission is to help cadets perform better in all three pillars of the Academy: academic, military, and physical.

To help in the academic arena, they offer a number of classes, all electives, to help cadets with study, learning, and time management skills. About half of cadets take RS101, a class that covers time management, note taking, test preparation, goal setting, and stress management.

The Center also offers a class in reading efficiency, which helps with speed and comprehension. According to the director, the class can help you double your reading rate. With time at a premium, that is a very helpful skill. They also offer a class in information literacy, which includes research and writing skills as well as critical thinking.

ASKING FOR HELP

Every West Point cadet, graduate, and professor will tell you that help is there for you if you just ask. Asking for help can be hard to do, especially since you may never have been in need of extra help before. The sooner you change that way of thinking, the better off you will be.

The professors at West Point take pride in being available to help cadets. While some have limited hours available for Additional Instruction, most will go well out of their way to find time to give you extra help.

Said one upperclassman, "As soon as you leave class and feel behind, get help. I've had teachers meet me at 8 p.m. They're always available. They'll give you their cell phone number, or have you over to their house. They're so committed to helping you pass class. As long as you're putting forth the effort, they'll do everything for you."

Cadets jokingly call those who require frequent Additional Instruction, "AI Rangers." Better to be an AI Ranger than an ex-cadet. A firstclass cadet said, "All it takes is a simple, 'Sir, I don't understand what we're going over today. Can we get together for a little while?' And you'll put your schedules together, figure out a time that's convenient for the both of you, and meet in his office for 20 minutes or an hour if necessary. My first two years I lived in my math instructor's office, especially as time came close for the exam."

Some cadets are more comfortable asking other cadets for help. Said a first classman, "Get all the help you can in your company. Your peers are best. There's bound to be somebody who's good in the class. If you are poor in the class, then you can always look to somebody that catches on. Then, there's other times when you catch on and you need to help somebody else. You can't survive here without getting help from each other. There's no way. If you can't get help from your friends, use your chain of command and get a tutor. That's the system here and we want them to use it."

A plebe explained that some cadets are reluctant to ask for help: "Most people come from the top of their classes. They're not used to being the ones who need help. My roommate is an example. She's about to quit because she's failing four subjects. It's kind of a combination of she didn't want to ask her peers for help, and she plays on company intramurals and her coach wouldn't excuse her until she was failing. I'll just send out a little e-mail to the other plebes saying I'm going to be in the study room working on this subject if you want to come by and ask a question. A lot of people will come. Actually, I've found that tutoring helps me a lot. I learn better, especially the math."

The general consensus is that, if you fail, it is because you gave up. As a firstclass cadet said, "You have to work pretty hard at failing out, because there are unlimited resources to help you."

As a final note, some of the cadets caution against doing the minimum to get by. Don't think that you can merely survive academically during your plebe year, then "fix" your GPA later. The classes will get harder, the time constraints will continue even though the demands will be different, and "plebe grades count."

CHAPTER **18**

Teamwork

If you are a serious contender for an appointment to West Point, you are probably used to being something of a superstar. You get the best grade on the test, you get elected president of the club, you set a new school record in your sport. You are generally known as someone who does well at whatever you take on.

That success was not given to you; you earned it. You work hard. You set high goals. You have made good choices about who your friends are and how you spend your free time. Peer pressure has limited effect on you. In other words, individual effort and individual thinking made you who you are.

One of the first things the Academy will try to change about you is that individual way of thinking.

GOODBYE TO INDIVIDUALITY

As the Vice Dean explains, you will have to "look for opportunities to be a member of a team. Many plebes have succeeded [in high school] because of their own individual efforts. Here, you have to appreciate being part of a team."

If you stand out from the crowd at West Point (especially during CBT), chances are you are doing something wrong. Why?

At West Point, as in the Army, most tasks are shared responsibilities. You would not want to go into combat next to someone who was concerned about looking good and getting all the credit. You would not want to go into combat with someone who only took care of his own needs and duties, and refused to help out a fellow Soldier. You would want to go into combat with a group of people who thought and worked as a single unit. One of the major objectives of CBT is to change your mindset, so that thinking as part of a team is automatic.

At the Academy, your own success will be tied to

West Point will teach you to think as part of a team.
United States Military Academy

your unit's success. If you set out on a five-mile road march, success will be defined as every member of your team completing the march. If someone else drops out, even if you completed it successfully, you have failed. Said one upperclassman, "You will always be judged by whatever group you belong to." (In the classroom, of course, your grades will normally be earned individually; however, your professors will often assign group projects and encourage study groups.)

One phrase you will hear from the upperclassmen is, "Square away your roommate." If your roommate's uniform is wrong, or if he or she is late for formation, it is your fault too. In fact, if you have the right uniform on or came to formation on time without them, you are even more at fault than your roommate—you knew better, but you only took care of yourself. That is seen considered worse than the plebe who made a mistake.

Cadets have several colorful terms for not taking care of classmates, none of which will be printed here. We will just call it "screwing over" your classmate, and it is considered one of the worst, most selfish things a plebe can do.

From day one of CBT, you should not think about how well you are doing, but on how you make your classmates successful. "It's like magic," says a colonel on the military instruction staff. "When you focus on helping your buddies, you won't worry about yourself. If you focus on yourself, you may not make it. You have to be a member of the team—you don't get to go home at the end of practice!"

Be prepared to let go of that fierce, determined individualism that served you so well in high school. If you have played team sports, you have had practice in the same kind of teamwork emphasized at the Academy. When you start thinking like a member of a team, life at the Academy will be much easier for you.

CLOSE QUARTERS: GETTING ALONG WITH ROOMMATES

You will probably share a room with one or two of your classmates. You may not have any say in whom you room with, especially as a plebe. Nevertheless, you will depend on each other to help get your room and uniforms in inspection order. You may help each other with homework if one of you is stronger in a subject than the other. You will help cheer each other up when one of you is feeling down.

If one of you is not pulling your weight, or you have a disagreement or personality clash, the plebe year could be much harder. So all cadets will tell you to resolve those clashes as soon as possible.

Probably the worst scenario is a roommate who cannot pull his or her share of the load. Said one cadet, "As a plebe, my roommate struggled with following regulations. She couldn't learn [knowledge]. We were always getting yelled at. I tried to help her out." A weak roommate is definitely a liability, but you will make the best of the situation if you take time to try to teach your roommate and keep him or her out of trouble.

One plebe figured out very quickly that a situation like this takes extra patience. "One of my roommates isn't clean or organized. I had to learn to tolerate it and be patient. Sometimes I take a break and then come back. It's how you deal with it. West Point reflects society. Roommates are human."

You may have a roommate who is annoying to you. Most cadets advise that you be proactive and deal with the issue, rather than try to ignore it. Said one upperclassman, "There are inconsiderate roommates. Stand up for yourself and say something to resolve it. That will drive you the least crazy." Explained another, "During the academic year, you can get away if you need to. Someone can always be gone from the room."

But most agreed that roommates will instinctively be respectful toward one another. They encourage you to talk openly about anything that is bothering you, and be direct about what you like. In most cases, roommates become your strongest allies: "You're stronger together as a team than you are alone. We have each other's backs. Helping each other out is the only way to be successful. We earn each other's successes."

And the Golden Rule applies when your teammate is less than ideal. "Be gracious when someone makes a mistake. They will do the same for you sometime."

FRIENDS FOR LIFE

Teamwork at West Point and the Army is much more of a plus than a minus, as you read in many of the graduate interviews in Chapter 3. Said one plebe, "Getting to know the people in my company has been the best thing. Your company is family while you're here. They are very protective of you; they actually care."

While you are a cadet, your friends will help you through your down days. Said an upperclassmen, "Remember, no matter what you're going though, there's someone else who has gone through it. Put out feelers and find them. Someone will remind you why you came here. Depend on your friends."

Cadets form very strong bonds with one another, especially their roommates. More than one struggling cadet decided to stay at West Point because they could not bear to leave the close friends they developed at the Academy. Those bonds last far beyond the four years as a cadet, even beyond a long Army career. Your friends from West Point will be friends for life.

CHAPTER 19

Advice for Intercollegiate Athletes

You have already read that the most stressful part of being a cadet is managing your time, allocating enough time and attention to the competing demands and requirements placed on every cadet. If you plan to be an intercollegiate athlete, you may have already wondered how the demands of practices and games or meets could possibly fit into this already packed schedule.

If you have talked with fellow athletes who are already playing at a civilian college, you may have a sense for what their lives are like. They may take 12 semester hours, or four classes, arranged to accommodate their practice schedule. Some days they may have only one or maybe even no classes, so they can focus 100 percent on their sport. On weekends when they aren't traveling, they may sleep late or catch up on their studies.

That's not the way it is at West Point.

About 30 percent of cadets are on the "Corps Squad," the collective term for all intercollegiate athletes. They represent the Military Academy in 17 different sports. After arranging their rooms in inspection order and attending breakfast formation, cadet athletes head off to class. They may be taking 18 or 21 hours in a semester, and like all cadets, they take the tough classes like physics and engineering. As soon as their last class is over, they go straight to practice or team meetings, getting back to their rooms to study as late as 7 or 8:00. Part of the weekend may be spent on military duties and training, or at least catching up on studies.

Athletes often miss out on opportunities to go home that other cadets have, such as spring break or Thanksgiving. Said one, "We don't get any three-day weekends because we always have practice." Unlike their civilian counterparts, cadet athletes will spend a good portion of every summer in military training programs, perhaps traveling around the country or overseas as part of their training. After they graduate, they will have a five-year commitment to serve in the Army, just like their classmates. They will face the realities of deployments and combat, and have few opportunities to pursue a professional athletic career.

If their lives sound extra demanding and difficult, they are. So why do they do it? Why not go to State U instead?

WHY ATHLETES CHOOSE WEST POINT

Nearly every cadet we interviewed gave roughly the same answer for choosing West Point: to become an officer and serve their country in the military. Sports are just a bonus, something extra. For some, sports helped them get an appointment to West Point. About 15-

20 percent of cadets are recruited athletes, and having an Academy coach on your side can definitely help the admissions process.

For many cadets, sports provide a distraction, a chance to do something they enjoy and are good at every day. Not every cadet has that opportunity. For the plebes, practice is a time when they can interact with upperclassmen informally, and feel a little more "normal." As one cadet explained, "Sports is a nice escape, a chance to feel more like a regular college kid for awhile." Another echoed that thought: "It makes me happy. I have a good attitude and it makes it easier here." A Corps Squad athlete, especially a plebe, will travel more than their classmates, and the change of scenery can be very welcome. And most enjoy the honor and responsibility of representing their Academy to other schools and the general public.

Some athletes come to West Point because it was their best chance to play on a Division I team. They weren't quite competitive enough to play at a "name" civilian college, but their strong leadership and academic credentials made them attractive to the Academy. So without a second thought, they accept an appointment to West Point.

However, within the first hour of the first day, the fact that they are at a military school becomes extremely clear. A few will decide that the military lifestyle is just not for them, and they will quit. On the other hand, many of those who arrive without having thought through the military service in their future will find that some of the same qualities that made them a successful athlete will make them a successful cadet—leadership, teamwork, discipline, competitiveness, determination, and endurance are all characteristics of a good Army officer. They will find that the camaraderie and esprit de corps of the military are as rewarding as being on a sports team. They will find it relatively easy to adapt to cadet life.

The Director of Intercollegiate Athletics explains, "I've been in the company of many officers who have commanded and led. They all say that graduates who participated in varsity athletics are some of the strongest leaders in the Army. They are molded to lead in pressure situations.

"So if you're interested, go on our website [look at both goarmywestpoint.com and usma.edu/athletics] and look at what we're about. West Point gives you many options. No place prepares you better for a career in the Army, the community, or in industry. If they see US Military Academy on your resume, you're on the top of the pile. "

A word of warning: if you eat, sleep, live, and breathe for your sport, West Point may not be a good choice for you. The Academy will require you to divide your time and attention among many competing demands, many of which have nothing to do with your sport. Being a cadet will actually keep you from practicing and focusing on athletics as much as you would like. Every day, as you shine your shoes or study for chemistry or line up in formation, you will be reminded that you are a cadet first and foremost.

Since 9/11, cadets receive an even more sobering reminder of what they have committed to. Every time a graduate is killed in combat, they pause to honor his or her service. They have no doubt that their service to country could come at a very high price. If you aren't ready to accept those realities, perhaps State U would be a better choice.

The gymnastics coach describes the recruiting challenge this way: "We are looking for energetic, articulate, outgoing young men and women. We want someone who can be successful. The opportunity to compete and travel as a Division I athlete is incomparable. West Point is a life changing opportunity you will remember for the rest of your life." If that sounds like the kind of opportunity you would like to pursue, read on.

HOW CADET ATHLETES MANAGE TO DO IT ALL

Time management. You may be tired of reading about how important it is for cadets. But for cadet athletes, time management is even more critical. They must learn to prioritize and make every minute count. They have to take advantage of a free period during the day to get some homework done, or use Sunday afternoon to get ahead for the week. "Be smart about it. Figure out what you can take time away from." Do not let yourself fall behind, they say, because it is so difficult to get caught up. "Always bring homework on trips, and try to work ahead."

Many Corps Squad athletes claim that playing sports actually makes them more productive and efficient. Said one, "I get a week off from practice and I don't know what to do! In season, I always know exactly what I have to do." Another agreed: "I actually do less homework during the off season."

Many cadet athletes emphasized the importance of getting extra help and taking advantage of the resources available. The swim team captain explained, "Establish a relationship with your instructors and they will help you out. And if they see that you care [enough to spend time getting extra help], they look at you more positively. I had a teammate who went into the math final thinking she had a D in the class, but she had a C because the professor had given her instructor points."[1]

Extra resources are available specifically for Corps Squad cadets. A tennis player explained that officer representatives, professors in the more difficult subjects, often travel with the teams and hold study sessions during trips. A football player said that his team holds mandatory study sessions with professors present to answer questions. The coaches monitor cadets' academic progress, especially during the first two years, and make sure they take advantage of tutoring and extra help if needed.

The athletic department is proud of the support they provide: "The NCAA recognized that our programs help with athletes' graduation rates, and they want to look into what we do as a model for the rest of the NCAA."

Another word of advice from cadet athletes: "Make sleep mandatory. Your quality of life drops when you stop getting enough sleep. Consider it a mandatory activity." Another agreed, "Set a specific time, say 12:00, when you'll stop doing homework and go to bed." A final suggestion from a first class cadet: "Take it one day at a time. During CBT, just focus on getting through the next meal. During plebe year, just decide to get to the next holiday. Take it step by step, so you're not overwhelmed."

---

[1] Many course grading policies leave a small percentage of the total points to the professor's discretion. These points are awarded based on class participation, preparation, and also attitude and effort. They have nothing whatsoever to do with athletics—any cadet would be eligible for them.

CADET OR ATHLETE? WHAT COMES FIRST?

At West Point, cadets are constantly reminded that they are no longer individuals. They are part of the Long Gray Line, the Corps of Cadets, and the United States Army. Conformity, unity, and selflessness are part of the culture. This raises a question: Do the unique demands (and sometimes privileges) that athletes have interfere with being part of the larger team? How do athletes prioritize their sport and their team along with all the other very important demands of a cadet? And how do their non-athlete classmates perceive them?

From the non-athlete's perspective, the athlete may seem to lead a privileged life. He or she gets to eat lunch and dinner with their team instead of the company, and avoid the extra scrutiny from their upperclassmen. They may miss a Saturday parade or a military training event, and they get to travel when other cadets are trapped on post.

But these "privileges" come at a cost. Other cadets may head home over a long weekend, spend Sunday afternoon watching football, or get their homework done by 10:00. Meanwhile, the athlete is working furiously to make up the work he missed last week during the baseball trip, or spending part of Christmas break practicing with her basketball team.

Is there resentment between the two groups? According to one cadet, it is very important for cadet athletes to balance their time, and show their commitment to military training. There is some resentment, especially among plebes, because "a lot of people don't understand how much extra work [being an athlete] is." This resentment is fuelled by the fact that some plebe athletes "hide" — stay away from their company and military duties even more than their sport requires.

Cadets say that it depends on the company, because each company has its own personality and culture. Said one athlete, "There is some bias against plebe athletes because they're not there for duties. But some companies support their athletes and go to their sporting events, and the athletes try to be present in the company whenever they can." Said a football player, "In some companies, cadets talk behind the athletes' backs. But even though we aren't there for some of the duties or company activities, we're still working as hard as we can to make ourselves better. We're not sitting around doing nothing!

"A little animosity, because someone is trying to get out of training or a duty, hurts everyone and creates a gap between the Corps Squad athletes and non-athletes. I suggest you be as active in the company as you can. If you make the effort to do the little things, the tactical officer and the company will notice."

A non-intercollegiate cadet agreed: "When an intercollegiate goes out of the way to help, it means the world to your company." And another said some athletes "will take any chance to be excused and not help their company mates. But tons of them make a huge effort. Be transparent, and contribute as much as you can, or you will miss out on relationships with your peers."

Most cadet athletes feel accepted and respected by their peers. They take on leadership roles in the Corps and find ways to bridge the gap. One cadet summarized, "Everyone has to be open minded and understanding. There's not just one path to success as an officer." Several successful officers and cadets offer more insight and advice below.

MORE ADVICE FROM ATHLETES

General (retired) Ray Odierno, Class of 1976

After playing football and baseball at West Point, General Odierno became an artillery officer. He served in Operation DESERT STORM and the Balkans. He also earned a master's degree in nuclear effects engineering from North Carolina State University. He commanded the 4th Infantry Division in Iraq, where his unit was able to capture Saddam Hussein. General Odierno has served as Assistant to the Chairman of the Joint Chiefs of Staff, commander of U.S. Army III Corps, commander of the Multinational Force-Iraq, and Chief of Staff of the Army. He retired in 2015, and joined JP Morgan Chase as a senior advisor.

Growing up in New Jersey, one of the biggest football games of the year was the Army-Navy game, and I was always struck by the enormous sense of history, spirit, and camaraderie exuded by the Corps of Cadets, which was represented on the field by the football team. During my senior year of high school, as Coach Cahill sat in my living room and talked about coming to West Point, I realized I had an opportunity like no other. Choosing to go there was about challenging myself mentally and physically, but more importantly, it was about being part of something bigger than myself, joining a team, and serving my Nation.

I was impressed by the discipline and values that permeated the Corps of Cadets, the emphasis on selfless service, teamwork, and working together toward a common goal — something I loved about playing sports — that was so central to the Academy's mission: to build leaders of character for our Nation. It just seemed like a natural fit for me. At West Point,

General Odierno began his Army career as a cadet athlete, and ended it as Chief of Staff of the Army. *Courtesy Ray Odierno*

I realized that I would receive a world-class education, but I would also be challenged as a person and would mature and develop in ways that I would not at other schools.

There were some basic advantages [to being an athlete], such as Corps Squad tables and having the privilege to eat meals without harassment. But I have always maintained that an Army athlete is like no other. In the early seventies, there was no relief from your class schedule — to include Saturdays. You were given only minor advantages, and in many ways, athletes were expected to do more. Every cadet maintains an incredibly busy schedule, balancing academic requirements with company duties and military training. But athletes also have to squeeze several hours (at least) of practice every day into that hectic schedule, not to mention entire weekends away from the Academy when the rest of the Corps has time to catch up on the week's work. While athletes are excused from certain duties, I made every effort to be part of the 'team' of plebes in my company, as well as a part of the football and baseball teams.

Though playing sports made for a busy schedule, it provided an excellent respite from the challenging life of a plebe. On the field, I was able to return to doing something I loved, and I developed friendships that are still very important to me today.

It is always about friendships. I developed long-lasting relationships with my company mates, as well as my baseball and football teammates. We spent four formative years together. We all had the same challenges, and we worked together to handle them. I also had a tremendous advantage because my future wife lived in New Jersey and provided me incredible support throughout my cadet years. We were part of the "2% club" — we survived the four years of West Point together.

West Point has always had programs in place to assist all cadets. It is about you taking advantage of them. I have found that academic instructors and coaches at the Academy understand the unique demands placed not only on athletes, but on all cadets, and they are all willing to work with you. It is just a matter of reaching out for that help. I always found that if an instructor could see that I was truly making my best effort in class, he would work with me to help me through the class. As is the case with most cadets, there were plenty of all-nighters and many times when I waited until the last minute to finish an assignment.

Back then we carried over 21 credits a semester. The workload was enormous. It forced you to prioritize and make choices. There were some times when an academic paper or project wasn't quite as good as I would have liked it to be, but I was able to manage the competing demands on my time, and it taught me a great deal, both about time management and about myself.

Team sports provide a basis for several important developmental traits, beginning with selflessness, discipline, adaptability, teamwork, and perseverance. They require the ability to think and execute under physical and mental stress. These all translate to successful leadership traits and build in you an inherent mental and physical toughness necessary to function in complex, high-stress positions.

First, [I would tell candidates] it is an opportunity like no other. It is an opportunity to become part of something bigger than yourself. I'd emphasize that your first priority is to be successful as a cadet and to graduate as an officer in the US Army. Playing a sport is part of that development and will be a very rewarding aspect of your time at the Academy. Much will be expected of you, and in many cases you become the face of the Academy.

But always remember why you are there. Ensure you find ways to participate with your fellow cadets in some of the required activities — duties, drill, company tables — because ultimately, accomplishing those tasks, even though they seem menial and mundane, will help build character and a mutual respect between you and your classmates.

That said, enjoy the opportunity to play a sport and be part of a team; it is a tremendous experience. Find that balance between being an athlete and a cadet. The selflessness, dedication, and discipline you learn will make you a better person. West Point athletes are special leaders, given special missions, who will lead in our Army and outside our Army.

Lieutenant Colonel (retired) Kim Kawamoto, Class of 1992

Kim Kawamoto was born in Vietnam and raised in Hawaii. She played basketball at West Point, then entered the signal corps. After assignments in Korea and North Carolina, she became a company commander in Maryland. She served as senior woman administrator for NCAA athletics at West Point and was deployed to Afghanistan. She retired in 2013, and serves as athletic director of a private school.

I had never heard of West Point until my basketball coach gave me a pamphlet. I talked to one grad on the phone, talked to the coaches, and saw a horrible video. If I had visited, it probably would have scared me. But my dad knew about West Point and encouraged me to apply.

I enjoyed the physical aspects of CBT. For athletes it's easier, and I like that kind of challenge. Mentally, it wasn't that big a stretch from my upbringing. I was used to doing what I was told. But I thought it was stupid and I wanted to leave. I called my mom, and she said I'd lose my chance for a better life. I told myself I'd stick it out. There will be times you want to quit, but just take it day by day and stick it out.

I tried to be a good plebe. I wanted to be seen doing duties, and I tried hard to pull my own weight. I think I earned some respect during CBT. The other cadets appreciated that I could hang with them. I tried to be involved whenever I could. They knew I was working as hard as I could. You're tired as heck all the time. You give up your Thanksgiving leave, you never have a free weekend.

Our team struggled my plebe year. We were a young team, but after that, we were always ranked nationally. Winning gives you a positive outlook, gives you something good to focus on. It's tough to hang in there for four years, especially for the people who never even get to play, never take a snap.

Being on Corps Squad was challenging, but it helped me with time management. It forced me to look at my schedule and figure out how to make it all fit. Plan ahead. All the course syllabi are on the servers, so you can fully plan out the entire semester.

As an athlete, you have a built in support group. Without that, it would have been harder. The coaches watch out for you, mentor you, and track your progress. The type of folks we recruit at West Point are type A, go-getters. Then they get to the Academy and it's tough. You might feel stupid asking for help. But it's a lot more challenging until you learn to ask for help. Some athletes don't take advantage of all the help that's available.

As an Army officer, in every facet of leadership, being on a team correlates — pulling your own weight, being ready to step up and lead, commitment, teamwork. Belonging to a team, you understand your role and how to contribute. You can tell a lot about athletes, how they practice and how they play…that's the same way they are as people.

Cadet Olivia Fairfield, Class of 2017

Raised in Iowa as one of six siblings, Cadet Fairfield watched her older sister enter West Point with the class of 2014. She was recruited to play volleyball, and is currently team captain and leader of the Brigade Student-Athlete Advisory Committee, which is the "captain of captains" for the Corps Squad teams. She was named 2013 Patriot League Rookie of the Year and logged 23 career double-digit kill games. An environmental geography major, she is waiting to find out which branch of the Army she will serve in after graduation. Another sister is a year behind her in the class of 2018.

My older sister was a recruited athlete, and it turned out she loved it here. It fit her well. Then when I was recruited, I couldn't understand why anyone would want to spend their college years at a service academy. My dad told me just to visit before I made up my mind. As soon as I drove by Thayer and the library, I had this weird feeling that I had to go to school here. I love the institution and everything it stands for.

I attended USMAPS, and when I got there I was pretty overwhelmed. I didn't know about the military at all, and I was so nervous. When I started CBT, I already had 200 friends from prep school, and I knew what to do. The most challenging part was not being able to talk to one another, to communicate to get to know your classmates. So you form bonds by going through the physical stuff together and helping each other through it.

The academic year is pretty overwhelming as a plebe. You

Cadet Fairfield is co-captain of the West Point volleyball team. *Courtesy Cadet Fairfield*

have to greet everyone, and now there are 3,000 upperclassmen. As an athlete, I didn't have as much time as other plebes to get my room set up and get organized before classes started. So I was up late doing things like getting my bed made and my room ready for inspection. But prep school helped me learn how to organize my time and prioritize my work. Early on, I got behind in chemistry class because of travel and practice, but I had notes from prep school so I was ok.

The best thing about being a cadet athlete is being on a team and having 15 best friends who are going through the same things you are. You can talk to them, and you will have an incredible sense of support from teammates, coaches, and other officers who work with your team.

The hardest thing is missing opportunities with your company. I have such a good company. On weekends and evening, they do a lot of things together, and I have to miss them for practice or games.

Time is the most important thing at West Point, and athletes have even more demands on their time than others. Some cadets think athletes get out of a lot of stuff, but we have to miss a lot of opportunities, and we have less time for academics. There is tension between Corps Squad athletes and other cadets because of the stuff we get out of, such as parades and drill. Some of them do understand, but there is a divide, which is too bad.

I would tell any candidate that West Point is a good place to be only if you want to be there. You can't be there because of any outside influence, or you probably won't make it.

For plebes who are Corps Squad athletes, my advice is to do what you're supposed to do in your company area. Do your duties, call minutes, do a little more so non-athletes don't give you a hard time. Be present, help others out, and volunteer for duties. Spend your time wisely — don't waste time socializing. And be organized. When you're having a hard day, talk to your teammates.

West Point is hard, but if you want it, you can do it. It's an opportunity not many people get — the opportunity of a lifetime, with all the experiences you get. Doors will open up for you for the rest of your life.

CHAPTER 20
Diversity and Respect

If you look through an old West Point yearbook from the 1960s, you will see the faces of a brigade that was very homogeneous. First, all of the cadets were men. Second, few were black or Asian. Most were practicing Christians, or perhaps pretended to be every Sunday. If any of them were gay, they had to hide it with every fiber of their being, because if the fact were discovered, their Army career would have ended with humiliation, immediately.

Just as our society has evolved to be more appreciative of the gifts of a diverse population, West Point has changed as well. Looking at the class of 2019, women comprise 22 percent. The class of 1,270 cadets includes 189 African-Americans, 93 Asian-Americans, 119 Hispanic Americans and 10 Native Americans.

Religious beliefs among midshipmen are as diverse as the nation's as a whole. The Academy supports the spiritual needs of all faiths — Christians and Jews, Buddhists and Muslims, and nearly every other faith represented in our society. Agnostics and atheists are accepted as well. As one Academy chaplain explained, "At the beginning of Plebe Summer, we explain the concepts of religious diversity. We talk about the First Amendment, and the Navy's policy to protect the religious observances of members as much as possible. That's one of our core competencies as chaplains, to facilitate the free exercise of religion for all."

As for sexual orientation, the Clinton-era policy known as "Don't Ask, Don't Tell" ended in 2012, so the Academy now admits openly-gay cadets. Some are open about their sexual orientation, belong to the support group called Spectrum [does this exist at USMA, or just USNA?], and date. Others are more low-key for various reasons. But all now have the indisputable right to be part of the Brigade.

Does this mean there is no more intolerance, disrespect, or prejudice among cadets? Of course not. But the Academy is working hard to promote a climate of mutual respect for several reasons. First, they are developing cadets to become leaders ready to take on the demands of command and combat. Good leaders are those who are understanding and respectful of everyone they lead. Second, the taxpayers who pay for the Academy expect it. And finally, they know it is the right thing to do.

If you grew up in an area where everyone looked, worshipped, and thought pretty much the same, the Academy may be a bit of a shock. Many cadets, however, really enjoyed meeting and interacting with people whose experiences have been different from their own.

If you consider yourself part of any minority group, you may have concerns about how you will be treated or your chances for success. The best thing you can do is find a midshipman or graduate and ask about his or her experiences. The next best thing is to read the experiences of some of the people in this chapter.

Brigadier General Stephen Michael, Class of 1988.

General Michael was a combat engineering major at West Point. He became an infantry officer after graduating, and has served two tours of duty in Iraq, the first during the initial invasion, and most recently as commander of an infantry battalion. He served as a Regiment Tactical Officer, with responsibility for eight cadet companies — about 1000 cadets, and as a brigade commander with the 10th Mountain Division. Most recently, Michael served as the Deputy Director for the Pakistan Afghanistan and Transregional Threats Coordination Cell on the Joint Staff at the Pentagon. He is now assigned to the 25th Infantry Divison in Hawaii.

I was born in Guyana, South America and immigrated to the United States in 1979 at the age of 14. A week before graduation from Science High in Newark, New Jersey, I received an introductory letter from West Point. Believe it or not, I had never heard of West Point; however, given that Guyana was at one point a British Colony, my father had, and understood it to be similar to Sandhurst, the United Kingdom's military academy, and further stated that I should look into it. Upon graduation from Science High (1981) at the age of 16, I attended Essex County Community College and while there applied to the Academy. Given that I was not yet a citizen, I was offered admission to West Point's Preparatory School at FT Monmouth, New Jersey. Upon graduation from the Prep School I had only been in the U.S. for four years, and in order to be eligible for citizenship, I needed to be a permanent resident for at least five years. So I spent the next year at the New Jersey Institute of Technology and at the end of the school year, applied for my U.S. citizenship and received it in an expedited fashion in order to join the Class of '88 in the summer of 1984.

Michael when he was a regimental tactical officer. *Courtesy Stephen Michael*

I loved my time at West Point; it was, from my perspective, the best education available, and at no cost … and, it goes without saying that my time there was broadening and foundational; much of what I am today was a function of what was instilled in me during those formative years. Initially, it was about the education and the experience, and it wasn't until my second class year that I began to internalize the fact that I was going to be a lieutenant in the Army of the United States.

Having the prep school and two years of college under my belt instilled a level of maturity in me that allowed me to deal with the challenges and adversity, and maintain a healthy perspective and not take any of it personally. Physically, I was always a good runner, but I had to work a little to get up to speed on my pushups and sit-ups.

My prior college time was both a blessing and a curse, in that while it allowed me to validate some courses (at times I almost wished I hadn't), it led initially to a tougher academic schedule, like advanced math, for example. However, in the end it enabled much more options for electives. Overall, I was an average student, and more so by choice; I spent a lot of time focused on relationships (people) and extracurricular activities (Protestant Sunday School Teacher, and Superintendent my Senior Year; member of the Cadet Gospel Choir; a mentor working with a West Point Middle School activity called God's Gang, and others). For me, the value of West Point was the entire process and much more than just the phenomenal education, studying steel construction, thermodynamics, etcetera. It was taking 22 credits in a compacted college semester, the Military Science, full summers of military training, intramural sports, four years of Sandhurst, leading within the Corps, pulling a couple all-nighters a week my junior year, juggling multiple glass balls, and figuring where to assume risk because I could not do it all. All of that was the sum of my "education" at West Point, and it has enabled me now in the Army to thrive in adversity and do some of my best work under pressure.

Now given some of the issues that our nation is wrestling with, I am sometimes asked, what has my experience been as an immigrant and an African American. Looking back some 28 years ago, I never felt there was a problem because of the color of my skin. I'm not naïve enough to think that prejudice and racism did not exist, but I never experienced it. Later, as a Regimental Tactical Officer, there were instances that I became aware of within the Corps and at West Point. After all, racism is learned and is a problem of culture, in that it is a multi-year and generational problem that will require leadership at the community, district, state and national level to fully overcome. Looking back on my years on active duty, there are probably two instances where racism could have played a role; however, at the time I did not think so. Overall, to me, the Army is a meritocracy — if you show up and make the organization better, you'll do well and succeed. There are incidents of racism, but it is not widespread or institutionalized. Being close, a part of a unit, and sharing hardships breaks a lot of that down. Soldiers come from all over the nation, from all different backgrounds and walks of life, and at the end of the day we find out that we have a lot more in common than that which makes us different or sets us apart. That's the great thing about the Army; it exposes many of fallacies we come in with.

The Academy has been an opportunity of a lifetime, a world class education, more often than not rated amongst the top five engineering and public colleges in the nation…and it's free. West Point has expanded my horizons, and as we've famously said over the years, "Much of the history we teach was made by the people we taught;" once you graduate and serve you will do things others can only dream or imagine.

Cadet Sean Deaton, Class of 2017

Cadet Deaton grew up as a proud "Army brat," and wanted to serve as his father did because he appreciated the Army lifestyle, and he hopes that his service increases the chances that his own children will never need to serve in the military. A computer science major, he plans to serve in cyber security or the Signal Corps after he graduates. He is the Cadet in Charge of Spectrum, West Point's gay-straight alliance club. He also developed an app called "The Poop Deck," which helps plebes learn required knowledge.

When I was in high school and first applying to West Point, I figured I could hide [my sexual orientation] for four years. I knew it would be worth all the benefits, and I really wanted to serve. I was a little worried, but I was prepared to deal with it.

I actually turned down an appointment right out of high school and went to civilian college for a year. I wanted to see what civilian life was like, having lived all my life on Army posts. That year helped me succeed here. It helped me know for sure West Point was the right choice for me.

Cadet Basic Training was tough, but I thought it was well planned out. It was actually more pleasant than I expected. I could tell the cadre cared about us, about our training and what we would get out of it. The hardest part was all the changes you have to get accustomed to — having roommates and living in close quarters, eating when you're told to eat, sleeping when you're told to sleep. Fortunately, the training is tailored to people at different levels of fitness. For example, for runs you are grouped by speed and ability. There are some parts of CBT you can't train for — ruck marching, running with heavy equipment on, but I found it all very doable.

Cadet Deaton celebrates getting his class ring.   *Courtesy Sean Deaton*

I thought the academic year was better than training in the field. You have a lot more freedom to do what you want to in day-to-day life. My year of college helped prepare me for academics; I had better time management skills. On weekends, I would hang out with friends or go to New York City.

By the time I started my plebe year, the law [Don't Ask, Don't Tell, which obligated LGB service members to keep their sexual orientation secret] had changed. I saw that as positive. At first I thought people's attitudes wouldn't have changed. But when I got here, I realized people are far more accepting than I expected. I told some of my squad mates I'm gay during basic training. They were all totally accepting. That has been my experience here, for the most part. It has been overwhelmingly positive.

My advice to candidates is to have the whole package when you apply. Don't focus too much on one thing, such as sports or academics. The Army needs you to be a well-rounded leader, someone with integrity and character. Don't be too worried about what it will be like here; this place is great for all the reasons you think it is. And regardless of your sexual orientation, it's far more accepting than you'd think, so there's no need to worry.

Dr. Rasheed Hosein

Dr. Rasheed Hosein is the officer in charge of the West Point Muslim Cadet Association. He has been teaching Western Civilization and Middle Eastern history at the United States Military Academy since July of 2011. He holds a doctorate from the Department of Near Eastern Languages and Civilizations at the University of Chicago.

At any given time, approximately 30-40 Muslim cadets attend West Point. Most are Americans, while a few are foreign exchange cadets from Muslim countries. As the officer in charge of the Muslim Cadet Club, Dr. Hosein helps coordinate with West Point leadership to craft policies and exceptions to protocol so that Muslim cadets can practice their faith. For example, when Ramadan (which requires Muslims to fast during the day) falls during summer training, West Point has allowed Muslim cadets to reschedule some of their training. He helps them obtain excusals from classes during Muslim high holidays, and arrange for prayer space. The group also gathers on Tuesday nights for social events, scripture study, and other activities. On Fridays, they gather for congregational prayers.

According to Dr. Hosein, the Academy leadership has been "more than willing to accommodate" the needs of Muslim cadets. They try hard, he says, to come up with solutions whenever conflicts or issues arise. What about the other cadets, especially at a time when terrorist attacks are linked to Islamic extremism? Social media can sometimes get ugly at West Point, just like it does other places. Occasionally cadets will speak without thinking first, saying disrespectful things to Muslim cadets. But according to Dr. Hosein, "We try to turn those into teachable moments." He feels that understanding is increasing, and ignorance and stereotyping are decreasing among cadets as they interact with Muslim cadets.

Overall, he says he would tell Muslim candidates and their families that West Point is a "good environment and a good place to be."

Chapter 21
Have Fun

By now you have grasped the message that succeeding at the Academy requires a lot of hard work, and it will often be stressful, difficult, frustrating, and exhausting. Most of the survival tips in this book, so far, have focused on how to meet these difficulties successfully and overcome the challenges by using your efforts as efficiently as effectively as possible, and asking for help along the way.

You may think that having fun is not part of the Academy experience. You may think, "If every minute of the day is so precious, how could there be time for fun?" However, nearly every cadet and graduate interviewed offered this piece of survival advice: do something for fun, something you love, something that relaxes you or makes you feel confident or just plain happy.

Rugby is one of many club sports at West Point.   *United States Military Academy*

You may be wondering, given the highly structured military life at the Academy, "How does a cadet have fun?" This chapter will give examples of the many enjoyable clubs and activities the Academy offers to help balance the rigors of cadet life and make the time pass more quickly.

CLUBS

Like most colleges, the Academy offers a wide variety of clubs for sports, hobbies, and other special interests. Some clubs are competitive, including cycling, triathlon, powerlifting, and judo. Many colleges have a number of sports that lack NCAA status, but still have rigorous practice and competition schedules. Club athletes do not have all the same challenges and privileges of NCAA intercollegiate athletes, but their experiences are quite similar.

Other clubs are focused on hobbies, special interests, and community service, such as fly-fishing, paintball, or glee club. Still others relate to an academic area or an Army mission, such as foreign language clubs, Model United Nations, combat weapons, or small unit tactics.

Clubs provide you an opportunity to explore your interests and relate to other cadets in a more relaxed environment than the typical plebe day. You will interact with upperclassmen without getting yelled at, and they in turn will mentor you in a comfortable environment. You may also get to know an officer or NCO who can share experiences about life in the Army as well.

Clubs also can give you the opportunity to travel, which provides a much-needed change of scenery and a new perspective on life as a plebe. If you have some talent or expertise, clubs offer a chance to show off your abilities and gain some confidence. For example, a talented fourthclass musician can be a star in the Spirit Band, or an expert

Singing groups, such as the Knightingales, offer a chance to participate in something fun and travel off post.   *United States Military Academy*

horseman can shine in the Equestrian Club, even if he or she is struggling in chemistry or plebe knowledge.

Some cadets participate in Big Brothers/Big Sisters, visiting schools off post in the local community, while others belong to religious organizations or service clubs that take them beyond the gate.

One cadet advised taking advantage of West Point clubs to try new things: "Go to every table on club night. Try new things." Another warned about getting overenthusiastic about all the options: "Some plebes will overcommit, but they will learn quickly which one they need to drop" — because of time limitations.

RECREATION

The Academy offers many opportunities for recreational activities. For example, you can sign up for a ski trip or SCUBA trip, plus many other types of trips where you can "go places and do things a plebe couldn't otherwise do." In fact, as with clubs, you will find more appealing activities to participate in than you can possibly do.

Many cadets say a good workout is the best way to relieve plebe stress. If you find athletic activities relaxing, the cadet gym has racquetball, tennis, a pool, basketball courts, nearly anything you can imagine. Bikers and runners also have plenty of room to roam.

Eisenhower Hall Theater offers big-name shows, including plays and musicals, comedians, and musicians. You can also just organize a movie night and order in food with your friends.

Earlier chapters already mentioned sponsor families. They will provide you with another way to put a little distance between yourself and the Academy, if only for a weekend or an afternoon. Just being in a real house can be very relaxing. Another appealing getaway is visiting New York City, which is only 55 miles from the Academy, for plays, festivals, or just being a tourist. Many cadets mentioned taking advantage of the city's proximity, whether they had ever been there before or not.

What you do for fun matters less than the fact that you do something for fun. As one cadet explained, "You have to have something to look forward to during the week. I see some cadets working on papers on Friday nights, as if they don't feel comfortable about when to stop working. I have an informal rule: don't do homework on Friday night. Do nothing, relax, relieve stress."

Cadets are notorious for their intelligent sense of humor and creative pranks, which may be evidence of that need for fun trying to express itself. Especially during Navy or Air Force football weeks, the practical jokes played on cadets and officers from the opponent service are ingenious. You can go to YouTube and find plenty of funny videos cadets made to lighten up their day.

Some cadets cautioned that social media — Facebook, texting, email, etc. — does not count as socializing. You need to get out of your room and do something fun. Said one, "Facebook is not a substitute for time with your friends."

The bottom line? "Find something you're passionate about to do, something to look forward to and keep you grounded. You'll make friends outside your company, and it just helps you survive."

CHAPTER 22
Living with Honor

A cadet will not lie, cheat, steal, or tolerate those who do.

Every new cadet agrees to live by the Honor Code when they take the Cadet Oath of Allegiance at the beginning of Cadet Basic Training. The Honor Code binds all the cadets to a common purpose and sets the minimum standard for honorable living at West Point and, later, as officers in the U. S. Army.

In other words, if you decide to go to West Point, you also have to be prepared to live by the Cadet Honor Code and the system that implements it.

You may be thinking, "What exactly does this mean?" Rest assured that you will receive plenty of instruction and guidance concerning how the Honor Code applies. From the first day of CBT, you will get an education in the Honor Code. West Point leadership understands you are probably coming from a high school environment where cheating was common, and no big deal. They understand that your character development, as with the rest of your West Point experience, is a four-year process rather than an instantaneous change the moment you put on the cadet uniform.

The letter of the law described in the code is just the beginning. You will learn how to embody the spirit of the code, to live honorably and do the right thing. West Point is charged with developing leaders who treat others with respect, demonstrate perseverance and patience, and live a moral life worthy of the country's trust.

Said a previous Honor Committee chairman, "When the new cadets arrive, we spend a lot of time teaching them about the Code and the System. We believe those first hours of instruction are very important because they set the tone for the cadet's career."

Cadets must also understand the difference between violating a regulation and violating the honor code. For example, a new cadet smuggled a cell phone into his room, which is against regulations. When an upperclassman found the charger plugged into the wall, the new cadet was asked if he had a cell phone. The new cadet lied and said no. If he had told the truth, he would have received some sort of punishment, but by lying, he also committed an honor violation. As one cadet explained, "You can play games with the regulations — that's a part of cadet life. But you don't play games with honor."

Cadets and graduates of West Point will tell you that the toleration portion of the Cadet Honor Code is often the most difficult for most cadets to grasp. A cadet who knows about an honor violation is obligated to turn the offender in or see that the offender turns himself in. In the cell phone case above, the new cadet's roommate knew about the lie and failed to

You will be expected to live by the honor code 100% of the time.
United States Military Academy

come forward, and therefore committed an honor violation himself. Dr. Jeffrey Peterson, Chair for the Study of Officership at the Simon Center for the Professional Military Ethic explains, "The toleration clause of the honor code is a significant obstacle. Cadets have a hard time confronting their classmates. They don't want to be a 'rat.' But they have to learn to hold each other accountable in order to maintain the trust between the Army Profession and the American public."

The following scenario is probably a more typical plebe honor situation:
Cadet Smith has a history paper due on Friday, and although she has done some of the research, she hasn't started writing as of Wednesday. On Wednesday night, her roommate comes to her in a panic asking for help with chemistry. Then she remembers she got yelled at during lunch because her shoes weren't shined, so she spends 45 minutes working on her shoes. By the time she starts working on the paper, she is exhausted, and gets only half of it done.

Thursday night rolls around, and Cadet Smith is feeling under the gun. She looks online and finds a paper that deals with her topic. She copies several paragraphs into her paper, adds a healthy quantity of her own words, but does not document her source. She is satisfied that her paper will get a passing grade.

Cadet Smith has violated the Cadet Honor Code by cheating — presenting the work of the original author of those copied paragraphs as her own work. Intentional plagiarism constitutes cheating under the Code. According to a former Brigade Honor Officer, this is the most common honor code violation for plebes. They are comfortable with the information age and doing research on the internet. They know a lot of "resources" are out there. They also tend to struggle with time management, and fall behind. And before they know it, they are facing allegations of an honor violation. (And by the way, probably get an F on the assignment as well.)

Cadets will then conduct an investigation. Depending on the outcome of that investigation, the case could result in an honor hearing before a panel of nine cadets. About 65 cases a year are referred to hearings by the Commandant; about 22 of those will admit to the violation and attend an abbreviated hearing called a Cadet Advisory Board; about 15 per year will be found guilty during the hearing. Those found guilty can either resign, or face the possibility of being expelled by the Superintendent, the commanding general of West Point. However, in most cases, the Superintendent will grant discretion to a cadet who is found guilty, enroll them in a rehabilitative Honor Mentorship Program, and delay their graduation for either a semester or a year. Finally, the Superintendent could enroll the cadet in the Army Mentorship Program which requires the cadet to serve as an enlisted soldier for two years before seeking readmission into the Corps of Cadets.

One factor the Superintendent will consider is how much time the cadet has spent under the Code — is the offender a plebe or a first classman? Plebes are more likely to be granted a second chance. On the other hand, a first class cadet should know better and may face a harsher punishment. Other factors include whether the cadet turned himself in and cooperated with the investigation.

One possible outcome is that she be directed to complete a special leadership development program with a tutor — to analyze, discuss, and understand where she went wrong.

The intricacies of the system are less important than realizing that less than three percent of cadets ever become embroiled in honor cases. That's because the overwhelming majority believe in and embrace the Code; they all manage to live under the Code for four years — and beyond — with no problem.

How Cadets Feel About the Honor Code

Most cadets and graduates will tell you that living under the Honor Code is a wonderful way to live. Said one of the officer supervisors, "I would tell a candidate that the Honor Code is something to look forward to. You will actually be able to live in an environment where you can leave your wallet on your desk and find it on your desk the next day. I ride my bike to work. I have for the past three years. I have left it unlocked in the cadet area for three years. It's always there when I go home. That is a wonderful environment. Living with the Honor Code is not something to fear, or something to merely survive. It's something to look forward to and feel proud about." Imagine doing that at State U!

At West Point you don't have to second guess if someone is telling the truth. If a cadet misses class, the professor can ask, "Where were you?" The cadet replies, "Sir, I was at sick call at the hospital," and there's no doubt in the professor's mind. The same relationship exists among cadets. If they ask somebody a question, they know they are getting an honest answer.

The current chairman of the Cadet Honor Committee echoed this thought: "Cadets sometimes appear cynical on the surface, but most of them follow the code and hold it dear. They really do appreciate the unique opportunity to be around people you can trust."

Does the average cadet agree? Most of them — and this is a good thing — say they don't really have to think about the Honor Code, because it's just naturally how they have come to live.

Here's what some of them had to say:

An upperclassman remembers the Code as being a bit overwhelming at first: "At first, you're scared. You think, 'No way I'm going to graduate. It's too hard.' When I wrote my first paper, I was nervous about making a mistake in the citations. But it's really hard to break the code or cheat by mistake. They're not trying to get you."

Another cadet agreed: "Things that were acceptable in high school are not [acceptable here], like white lies. We're held to a higher standard, and it's kind of a shock. It takes a year or two to accept it. By your junior year, you're expected to get it. You realize why it's important.

"As a plebe, they set you up for success. Everyone takes the test at the same time. By the time you're an upperclassman, teachers will leave the room [during a test] and expect you not to cheat."

What about the toleration clause? Most cadets agree it is the hardest part of the Code to live by. They have a profound sense of loyalty to their friends and classmates, but as they mature they realize that their loyalty to the institution is stronger: "No one wants to see other lying or cheating around them. If they lie in war, even worse things can happen."

Some feel the toleration clause is not as well accepted as the rest of the code, which confirms the observations of the ethics and leadership faculty. An upperclassman explained that turning in another cadet for a violation is "viewed as ratting someone out. They tell you about toleration, but some don't seem to believe it. I think it depends on the [severity of the] violation."

Another offered this perspective of toleration: "It's a maturity thing. Is your loyalty with the organization or your friends? [Turing someone in] is about improving the organization, not protecting yourself."

The majority of cadets interviewed echoed the sentiments of this cadet regarding living under the code: "It's hard not to follow it. As long as you're doing the right thing, you don't have to worry. If you have doubts about something, it's probably not something you should be doing.

Here are some cadets' final thoughts about living under the Honor Code:
- It has become a way to live my life, so I don't have to think. It's just natural.
- In our career field, everything needs to be honorable. The code applies to something real, and it makes sense now.
- As a firstclass cadet, it is really ingrained. Life is better with it.
- At first it was scary. I was afraid of getting caught doing something stupid. Now, honorable living goes beyond the code itself, and the red flags are automatic.
- It's what makes us better than a civilian institution. I'm proud of that!

CHAPTER 23

The Realities of Combat

Throughout the 1990s, cadets at West Point trained to become combat leaders, just as they do today. But the possibility of experiencing actual combat was a bit more abstract then, a more remote possibility. Ten or fifteen years ago, there were professors and other officers at West Point who had combat experience, but those were relatively few. From time to time, cadets heard about graduates who died in training accidents or even military operations, but not very often.

Since 9/11, all that has changed. Lengthy deployments to austere or dangerous environments can be considered a near certainty in all cadets' futures. Today's cadets began the application process after the Army's involvement in Iraq and Afghanistan began. They saw the news and heard the stories. Many of them had long conversations with concerned parents, conversations about courage and patriotism and even fear. In other words, they knew what they were getting into.

Even though the OPTEMPO — the amount of time spent on deployments — has decreased somewhat over the past few years, the requirement for Soldiers to deploy into combat situations remains. You should be fully aware of what you are committing to after you graduate, and how that commitment will affect your time as a cadet.

TRAINING: MORE COMPLICATED AND MORE INTENSE

How has the current combat environment affected training at West Point? According to the officers that oversee this training, they are teaching many of the same basic competencies, basic principles of warfighting, employing weapons, combat first-aid and communications procedures. The list of required skills has not changed much over the years. However, now cadets must attain a greater level of mastery, because they may not have time after graduation to hone these skills. The Academy also works harder to make this training as realistic as possible.

This philosophy of training is designed to better prepare cadets for the complicated environments today's solders will encounter. Graduates will soon find themselves in situations that they could not have expected, planned, or trained for. They have to be creative and innovative, using what they have and what they know to solve problems.

So the newest combat skill is critical thinking. According to the officer in charge of military instruction, "[Training] situations are intentionally ambiguous. There are no black-and-white situations with right and wrong answers. The focus used to be what and

You will get combat training in both practical skills and critical thinking. *United States Military Academy*

how, but now we include the why. Cadets learn to think, solve problems, and communicate effectively."

You will practice skills such as how to clear a room, move tactically — both on the streets or through the woods, and be part of a tank crew. The training will get more and more advanced over your four years as a cadet. During their senior year, cadets rotate through leadership positions and practice solving tactical problems in "realistic, complex situations."

The Physical Education department has made some changes as well. For example, some of the courses that teach combat skills have been moved from the first or second year to the third or fourth, so those skills will be fresher when a graduate reports to his first unit. According to the director, first class cadets now take combat applications at the end of their cadet careers, rather than a recreational sport such as tennis or golf because "they are going to be warriors in combat."

EDUCATING CADETS FOR COMBAT

In Iraq and Afghanistan, and wherever the next military challenge lies, Army officers have to build trust, gain understanding, and create productive working relationships with people from very different cultures. They need to be comfortable, know what and what not to do in these complex situations. As a result, within the academic curriculum, the most obvious change is the increased focus on foreign languages and cultural awareness.

Each summer approximately 550 cadets will have the opportunity to go abroad on mini internships for three to five weeks. They may be engaged in remote areas of Africa, visit German battlefields, or help out a community in Thailand. The Academy has increased tenfold the number of cadets who study abroad for a semester — about 150 cadets in 16

The realities of facing combat after graduation will confront you regularly.   *United States Military Academy*

different countries each year. This semester allows them to take courses taught in another language, and become immersed in another culture.

The Academy has also added some new courses of study related to the contemporary environment. For example, cadets can now take regional studies or terrorism studies. One elective now offered is called Winning the Peace. This course covers everything from moral and ethical dilemmas to working with interpreters to collaborating with foreign agencies. One popular feature of the class allows cadets to interact with a Muslim community in nearby New Jersey. According to one of the professors, after they take the class, "When cadets see a Muslim woman covered, they no longer just see the cover. They see a real person. And the members of this community in New Jersey see the cadets as part of their family."

The PE department also educates cadets about life in a combat environment. During their third year, cadets take a class called Army Fitness Development that teaches them how to develop fitness programs for themselves and their units. They learn how to deal with factors such as heat, cold, fatigue, and the stress of combat environments.

Even in classes that have no direct application to combat, you may have professors who just returned from a tour in Iraq or Afghanistan. They will occasionally take time from a history lesson or a math class to discuss their experiences and answer questions. You will have plenty of opportunities to think and talk about the challenges you will face after graduation.

Said one cadet, "I came to West Point knowing we will all deploy. West Point is the best place to prepare."

THE RIGHT ATTITUDE

As with everything at West Point, the right attitude toward preparing for combat is critical. The perspective of cadets has changed because they know it's a matter of when, rather then if, they will lead troops into harm's way. How has this changed their attitude toward their time at West Point and their future as Army officers?

Cadets will tell you they view this responsibility as a very serious one. That means they focus on their military training, trying to learn as much as they can. They also take their leadership training more seriously, because they want to do the best possible job leading their soldiers — many will be in leadership positions, most likely as platoon leaders, within a year or two of graduation.

One upperclass cadet explained, "Every time a graduate dies, they announce it at lunch. As a plebe, it seemed far away, but now it seems more real."

Are they afraid? They certainly aren't afraid of taking on the toughest challenges. Graduates want to serve their country from the front, even if that means being in the most dangerous and demanding positions. As one cadet explained, "It makes me want to work harder, to make sure I can branch Infantry," because Infantry has become the most popular and competitive branch. (Branch choice is based on overall class order of merit.)

According to cadets we interviewed and the counselor who hears their concerns, there is only one thing that may cause them a little bit of fear: They fear that they will not be up to the task, that they will make a mistake, that they will let their fellow soldiers down. These are young men and women who want to do whatever their country asks of them to defend its values and freedom, and do it to the absolute best of their ability. They will do all they can while they are cadets to make sure they are ready.

Many cadets find their parents struggling with the reality of combat in the cadets' future. Some advise nervous parents to get with combat veterans through their parents club, and have an honest discussion about it. Others avoid talking about it altogether. You know your parents best, but if you become a cadet, you may one day need to discuss the risks of combat with them, how you have trained and prepared, and how you feel about it yourself.

Advice for parents — from the admissions process through the plebe year — is the subject of the next chapter.

Chapter 24

Advice to Parents

When their son or daughter is ready to leave for college, many parents are worrying about how to pay the tens of thousands of dollars in tuition, and how to keep track of the many scholarship applications. Parents of cadets do not have this worry.

On the other hand, parents must realize that getting an appointment to West Point and being a cadet are much more stressful and demanding than what a regular college student might experience. The demands on the parent are different as well. You will probably devote a lot of time, a considerable amount of anxiety, and lots and lots of moral support to your son or daughter.

This chapter for the parents of West Point candidates is a collection of advice for parents of candidates and plebes [first year cadets], starting with the admissions process and continuing on through the first year at the Academy. After your cadet survives the first year, there is not much more you will need to learn.

All of the advice comes from parents who have been there — parents whose sons and daughters have at least survived the first year at the Academy, and cadets who have definite ideas about how their parents should and should not help them. In addition, much of the advice is from parents who are, or have been, presidents of West Point Parents' Clubs. Their advice has extra value because, in addition to experiences with their own sons and daughters, they have helped numerous other parents cope with a variety of problems.

APPLY FOR THE RIGHT REASONS

During all the interviews, one bit of advice was heard over and over, and it was strongly recommended that it be the first advice parents of prospective candidates should here: Make ABSOLUTELY SURE that going to the United States Military Academy is your son or daughter's idea, not someone else's.

Nearly every officer who is involved with the admissions process had a story to tell about a young man or woman who went to the Academy because someone else wanted them to go. These stories never have a happy ending.

The current Commandant of Cadets — a general who is a 1980 West Point graduate, married to a graduate, and the father of a graduate — pleaded with us to make this point 100 percent clear. He shared sad stories of cadets who only came to West Point because a parent wanted them to. These cadets soon find themselves miserable, unmotivated, and probably failing. Even worse, when they call home for advice and support, they are sometimes told, "If you quit, don't bother coming home."

The never-ending demands, high levels of stress, and constant criticism they encounter at West Point require plebes to use every ounce of physical and mental fortitude they can muster, every single day. Said one graduate who is also a liaison officer[1], "You can't do four years of something you hate. You have to really want it."

So if a cadet is at West Point for someone else's gratification and not for their own reasons, they will surely end up quitting. They will have to carry the burden of that failure with them forever. And they will have ruined the opportunity for some self-motivated candidate who really wanted that appointment but did not get it.

As a parent, make sure you help your son or daughter examine their motives. Most parents who are graduates, when their son or daughter expresses interest in West Point, will stay detached, or even try to talk them out of it, just to ensure their son or daughter's motives are their own.

Another bit of advice is a logical extension of the preceding: Make sure that your son or daughter wants to go to the Academy for the right reasons.

Many parents and candidates are attracted by the fact that West Point is free, especially when the economy is doing poorly. Cadets laugh when you call their four years at West Point "free," because they believe they "pay" for it many times over with hard work and loss of freedom. If free tuition is the motivating factor, your son or daughter will soon decide it is not worth it.

According to many who evaluate colleges and universities, as well as many graduates and cadets, the Academy offers an outstanding academic experience. But if that is all that your son or daughter wants, it would be a mistake to go there.

The goal of the Academy is to produce leaders to serve in the Army. They will work long hours in the service of their country, and most will face the dangers of hostile fire and long separations from their families. A high quality college education certainly lies at the heart of the Academy program, but a whole lot more goes along with it.

The West Point education is above all a four-year officer training program. It is rigorous and demanding and requires young men and women to make great personal sacrifices, especially of their personal freedom. Prospective candidates should have firm goals that are in concert with the Academy's mission. If they want to become officers and serve their country in the military, after proving and improving themselves in a high-stress environment, then they stand a good chance of succeeding. It all depends upon how badly they want to achieve their goal.

However, if they are going for ANY other reason, or if their goal is not clear, perhaps you should suggest they look elsewhere. There are hundreds of high quality civilian colleges and universities where they can get an excellent education without enduring the rigors of the Academy. They can even try out ROTC to see if the military is right for them. And they also will avoid the emotional trauma that comes from being branded as a quitter, or the guilt and feelings of failure that come with being expelled.

Help your son or daughter examine why he or she wants to go to West Point. If their motivation is legitimate, they will have a much better chance of getting in and graduating.

[1] Military Academy Liaison Officers. or MALOs, interview candidates and advise them on the admissions process.

Sue Ross

West Point offers a first-class education, but it is also an officer training program.

United States Military Academy

KNOW WHAT THEY ARE GETTING INTO

Parents are advised to do everything they can to enable a candidate to learn as much as much as possible about the Academy. This will allow them to prepare academically, physically, and (most of all) mentally for the task ahead. The following is a variety of suggestions on how to achieve that goal.

A highly-recommended program is called Summer Leaders Experience. Students can apply for SLE beginning in December of their junior year of high school. If selected, they attend a week-long program at West Point during the coming summer. The program offers leadership and academic programs, as well as valuable exposure to the campus and cadet life.

Selection for SLE is even more competitive than an appointment to West Point. If your son or daughter is selected and continues with the application process, there is a very good chance that he or she will receive an appointment the following year. You will have to spend about $400 plus travel expenses, which includes room, board, and supplies. More information about SLE is available in Chapter 8 and at usma.edu/admissions.

West Point also provides a number of opportunities for you and your son or daughter to receive briefings and a tour. Available during the summer as well as the academic year, candidate visits can be arranged by visiting the admissions web site.

A third alternative is to attend a sports camp. The Academy offers week-long programs in a variety of sports. You will have to fund the travel expenses and registration fees.

While not specifically geared for potential candidates, the camps provide a chance to see the Academy up close. Schedules and registration information can be found at **www. goarmysports.com**.

If you live too far away or simply cannot afford a visit to West Point, do not worry. There are other ways to do research about the West Point experience. Find a West Point graduate who lives in your area. The high school counselor may be able to connect you with a cadet who graduated from your child's school recently. Also, many areas of the country have active parents clubs, and their officers understand the importance of prospective candidates getting advice from cadets and graduates. They, too, will help arrange meetings.

The bottom line is that every option should be pursued to learn more about the Academy beforehand, and to gain understanding of what it means to be a military officer.

THE ADMISSIONS PROCESS

Getting admitted to West Point is a three-step process, a process more involved than applying to Stanford or Georgia Tech. Many candidates eliminate themselves because they fail to complete all three steps.

The first step is becoming a candidate.

The second step is obtaining a nomination — a process unique to the service academies.

The third step is completing the application and obtaining an appointment. The procedures for accomplishing these steps are explained in earlier chapters. However, there are some things that parents should and should not do, according to the parents, cadets, and officers who were interviewed for this chapter.

One of the problems parents should be aware of is the bad information that candidates can receive when they initiate the admissions process. This is a troublesome problem because the information often comes from those whom one would expect to be authoritative — counselors, teachers, and administrators. An Idaho mother and parents' club president commented on this problem:

"These kids can get a lot of erroneous information about West Point, and it can come from people who seem to know what they are talking about. I'm speaking of people like their school counselors and their vice principal who can easily discourage kids with an off-handed comment like, 'Oh, you can't get into West Point unless you are in the top ten percent of your class or unless you have a 3.5 GPA.' I advise parents not to listen to things like that. Don't let someone like that discourage your kid. Mine was told that, yet he ignored what they said and got in with less than a 3.5 and I know now that there are many others who have done the same."

Encourage your son or daughter to do thorough research, including becoming very familiar the admissions web site, and talking to everyone they can find who has firsthand experience with the West Point admissions process. What else can you do?

Offer Help

Parents need to be aware of the complexity of the admissions process. The candidate has to fill out forms and write letters and essays. Also, senators and congressmen have their own unique procedure for applying for a nomination — procedures involving letters, documents, deadlines and, perhaps, appointments for interviews. Most parents believed that high school seniors need help with the logistics of the process. Following is a typical comment, which came from a Minnesota mother and parents' club president who has been through the process three times — twice for sons at West Point and once for a son at the Naval Academy:

"I really believe that most kids need help from their parents during the admissions process. That senior year in high school is really overwhelming — the typical candidate is heavily involved in athletics; they're taking advanced courses and have a heavy study schedule; they're in clubs and community organizations; they're taking the SAT and ACT; and, in addition, they don't have experience managing paperwork and keeping track of deadlines.

"I think that parents should help them to become organized. A mother can do things like help them with a master schedule so they know when everything is due. She can also help with the filing so that there is a separate folder for each senator and congressman. The kid should write all the letters, of course, but there is nothing wrong with helping them get the letters typed. Copying is another chore — the kid should keep a copy on file of everything that has been submitted, but making those copies takes time that most kids don't have.

"I remember when my first one started applying. We had no idea how much was involved and we learned that a kid can have problems if you don't help them with their appointments and deadlines. There are deadlines for everything and if they miss one of them that can be the end of it right there. The kid's tendency is to try to keep everything in his head. That is a bad mistake. Appointments and deadlines should be written down on a master schedule and everything else should be adjusted to them. And sometimes their appointments interfere with classes or their sports schedule, so it is up to mom and dad to talk to the school so the kid doesn't get in trouble for missing classes or practices."

A cadet we interviewed made a similar comment, "The application process is overwhelming. I needed help with things like making doctors appointments and getting letters from teachers. I also had my parents read over my application."

Another problem parents should be aware of is that many candidates are reluctant to follow up on the application process. The typical candidate thinks that once a high school teacher or administrator has been asked for a letter of recommendation, then that is all they have to do. They do not realize that those who are asked to submit letters often procrastinate past deadlines or fail even to write the letters.

Numerous congressional staffers spoke about this problem (they said high school principals were the worst offenders) and they strongly recommend that candidates follow up to make sure their files are complete. Of course, follow up is not something high school seniors are used to doing so it is important for parents to encourage the process. Several parents commented on other types of follow up that are important in the admissions process. An example is a comment from an Iowa father and parents' club president:

"Parents should constantly encourage the son or daughter to apply early and then follow up with both the Academy and the congressmen. By applying early they have time to overcome problems if they come up. Also, they have the opportunity to make what I call a communications trail. As the year progresses the candidate can update his files with his latest grades, an announcement that he has been elected to the student council, that he was voted captain of the football team, that he received an award for selling the most magazines, etc. This is important because, one, everybody [the Academy and congressmen] is looking for candidates with good credentials and, two, they are looking for candidates who really want to go to West Point. When the candidate follows up, this lets them know that he is serious — that he really wants it.

"I can cite our personal case to show the value of follow up. When our son applied, he was rejected by the medical review board out in Colorado Springs — the board that reviews candidate physicals for all the academies. His problem was that he had a history of two head injuries. One was a mild fracture when he was a child and the other occurred in junior high when he was hit above the eye with a baseball. The impact of the baseball made a slight indentation, which was corrected at that time by surgery. Well, with that on his record he was automatically rejected — I guess because they thought he was some kind of a risk.

"But our son did not accept that decision. He found out how to contact that board and he asked for a special review of his case. We also got medical statements from his doctors and some evidence to support the review, including an electroencephalogram. And all during the process he would pick up the phone and talk to the people in Colorado Springs, politely asking when his case was due for review, telling what new evidence he was submitting, etc. He also followed up the phone calls with letters saying that he appreciated the discussions and that he wanted them to know how much the opportunity meant to him.

"Later, when he was found medically qualified and notified of his appointment, I believe it was the happiest day in his life. I also believe that his persistence was a big factor in his success. I'm afraid too many candidates and their parents would tend to accept the review board's decision as being the end of the line. In my opinion, parents definitely should be advised to encourage the candidate to challenge anything they believe to be unfair."

Do not let your son or daughter get caught off guard by the timing of the West Point application process. The candidate application form can be filled out beginning mid-December of the junior year, although waiting until later in the semester will probably not cause any problems. However, most congressional offices require the nomination paperwork to be filled out early in the senior year, some by the end of October, and some as early as August.

If your son or daughter waits to settle into the schedule of senior year to get started, the opportunity to attend West Point may be lost — at least for the coming year. If they do not get a nomination, they will not get an appointment to West Point. Several cadets and graduates shared stories of attending prep school or college for a year before getting their appointment, simply because they got started on the application process too late. Encourage your son or daughter to get started early.

However, Don't Do It For Them

This is a good place, however, to warn parents against getting too involved in the admissions process.

Everybody who has anything to do with evaluating candidates, including congressional staffers, liaison officers, panelists and Academy officials, is looking for candidates who are victims of too much parental encouragement. They know from experience that candidates who want to attend West Point for any reason other than their own deep, personal desire are very poor risks.

Therefore, as a parent, try to stay in the background as much as possible. Help the candidate in the ways that have already have been mentioned. But when it comes to actual contacts with those who are involved in the admissions process, let your candidate do the actual writing or telephoning. Of course, it may be tempting at times to use your knowhow to solve a problem, but such efforts can backfire and actually hurt your candidate. Just remember that everyone evaluating candidates wants to have a good record — they want a high percentage of those they select to remain at West Point and graduate. Whenever they see a parent getting too involved, this is like a red flag warning them that the candidate's parents may be more highly motivated than the candidate. If your son or daughter really wants to go to West Point, do not let them think that of you.

Explained a liaison officer, "I saw one parent who controlled the entire process, a father who e-mailed me constantly with concerns and questions. Why didn't the kid e-mail me? Doesn't the father have confidence that the kid can do it? Candidates demonstrate commitment by doing it on their own."

One final bit of advice on the admissions process — encourage your candidate to apply to places other than West Point. If the young person is truly interested in an Army career, he or she should apply for an Army ROTC scholarship. Those with broader career interests should also apply for the Air Force and Naval Academies. In addition, each candidate should have at least one acceptance at a civilian college to fall back upon if the military options do not work out.

PHYSICAL PREPARATION

Most candidates are aware of the physical challenges of cadet life at West Point. They prepare with workouts designed to increase both their strength and endurance.

However, those who supervise incoming cadets say that some of them are inadequately prepared physically.

What should a parent do about this? Nothing, if your candidate is truly in top shape. But if you suspect that the opposite might be the case, encourage the candidate to do his or her own fitness test using the standards (numbers, times and distances) on the Academy's web site.

High school athletes sometimes overrate their physical condition — they think because they were good football or basketball players that the physical challenges at West Point will be a breeze. They may be really good at soccer and overall endurance, and have trouble with pushups and pullups and other tasks that require upper-body strength. If they work out according to West Point's preparation program, they can identify and correct their weaknesses before they report.

For women, this is even more critical. The surest way to earn the respect of the male majority is for female candidates to be in excellent physical shape when they arrive. Nothing impresses the men more than a gutsy woman who has the stamina to hang in there with them when the going is tough. On the other hand, nothing exposes women to more ridicule (often expressed silently or in very subtle ways) than when they have to drop out of a road march or give their pack to someone else to carry.

So if your daughter is headed to West Point, do whatever you can to help her get into excellent physical condition. The payoff will be huge, both for her psychological health as well as for her physical well being.

Appointees are also advised to show up with good, broken-in running shoes and combat boots. This will prevent blisters and sore spots when they show up for Cadet Basic Training, or CBT. You can help ensure they purchase these early enough to break them in.

One word of caution. Some of the candidates take the physical challenge too seriously and spend all their time after graduation worrying about getting in shape. Numerous cadets and parents cautioned that the weeks after graduation should also be used for fun and relaxation. To do otherwise, they say, is to invite a good case of the blues when, during CBT, the "new cadets" (that is what they are called until after the end of CBT) think back at all the fun their friends had that they missed. During CBT the new cadets have plenty of legitimate things to feel sorry for themselves about without the additional feeling that West Point caused them to give up a fun period in their life — a period that they will never have a chance to experience again.

THE R-DAY TRAUMA

Most parents had comments about "R-Day" (Reception Day), which is the early July day when candidates report to West Point. They report in the morning and, after a short ceremony, are told to take a minute and say goodbye to whomever may have accompanied them. Then they head off to get their haircuts, inoculations, uniforms and their first taste of military indoctrination.

Parents reported mixed opinions about whether or not the candidates should be escorted to West Point on R-Day.

The majority believed that if it is economically feasible, as many members of the family as possible should accompany the candidate on R-Day. They said that this is an expression of support that will sustain the cadet in the weeks ahead when the rough experiences of Beast Barracks are compounded by loneliness and homesickness. Also, they said that the lectures and tours that are arranged by West Point for that day helped them better understand the institution.

An example of the majority view is this comment from an Iowa mother and former parents' club president:

"We felt that it was very important for our son to know that his family was behind him so we made a family vacation out of it. We rented a motor home and took the younger kids, grandma and grandpa, and the girl he was going with at the time. It was a very good family experience for us, and while the parting was traumatic for us all, I think it was important for him to be sent off with love."

An example of the minority view is the following comment from a California parent who is also an official in a parents' club:

"He wanted to go by himself and I agreed because I think that if they want it bad enough, it is something that they should do on their own. Of course, it was very hard for me to see him go, and it is very hard on most parents. Luckily, when we got to the terminal, he met some others who were going back and that made it easier. If I had it to do over again, a few weeks before R-Day I would find out the names of others who are going from the region and try to get them together. The kids my son went with have since become very close because they have been riding the red1 eye specials together for the last three years."

Numerous parents spoke of the trauma they experienced on R-Day. But many said they would advise parents to try not to let their emotions show too much because the cadets are going to have it hard enough without worrying about the pain their parents are suffering. Said a mother from South Carolina who is the co-president of a parents' club:

"We have a parent in our club who says to this day, 'I just don't think I can stand it — it is just killing me not being able to see that boy.' My point is that it is very difficult for some parents. I went through the whole first year with my husband feeling that way. It was gut-wrenching for him, I mean really gut-wrenching because they had been so close. It literally almost made him sick.

Whether you accompany your son or daughter on R-Day or not, be sure to make the goodbye an emotionally-positive sendoff. *United States Military Academy*

"Psychologically it is like giving up your child, and I don't think some parents know how badly it is going to affect them until it happens. It is especially bad when a mother or father doesn't really believe in the kid's decision. I would say to parents that they should sit down during the application process and really talk everything over, then make sure the kid visits the Academy and talks to as many knowledgeable people as he can so he knows what he is doing. But once that decision is made and he says, 'Yes, mother and dad, this is what I want,' then it is important to support that decision even if it kills you inside!"

Another mom, who is a graduate married to a graduate, said this of R-Day, "It was a little stress for mom, but it's extremely well done, an emotionally powerful day. The parents seemed to be reassured. The Academy has a chance to explain things. The briefings are very good. It's a great first exposure, and there is so much information available. Later, we were able to spot our son in the parade, with his buzzed head, saluting. It was a great moment."

SUPPORT FROM HOME

Even the most highly motivated cadets will have problems and down times during the first year at West Point. The main problem is the abrupt transition from hearing nothing but accolades in high school to hearing nothing but criticism from the upperclassmen.

Before they left home, they were touted as outstanding young men and women. After their arrival at West Point they are instantly dropped to a status that would challenge the untouchables.

Before they left home their exemplary behavior had earned them freedom and respect. At West Point that freedom is suddenly taken away and no matter how hard they try, they seem not to be able to earn an ounce of respect.

While they are going through all of this, it is natural that they will feel lonely and depressed. So this is the time when parents are really needed, the time when parents need to mobilize the support brigade and do the kinds of things that will help their cadets' morale. It is the time when the cadets need to know that at least somebody loves them.

Here are the kinds of things parents who have been through it say you can do.

Said a father and parents' club president from Florida: "Those kids badly need to hear from home and we tried not to let a day go by when we didn't put something in the mail. They weren't long letters much of the time. They were just notes with little things — what the cat did or what trouble the dog got into. Sometimes we just sent silly things."

A mother from Rhode Island: "It is most important that they receive a barrage of letters. They don't have to be 12-page epistles. Just notes of what's going on, maybe with a daily comic strip, or a funny card or even a postcard — just so there is something in that mail box for them each day — even if it is a crayon drawing from the two-year old next door, it is important!"

A mother and past parents' club president from Ohio: "Letters are so very important but you have to be careful what you say. You need to write and keep them informed but don't make it sound like those at home are having too much fun. Already they are thinking about their buddies and things they are missing out on. You don't want to write and tell them all the things they are missing — that we did this and that and had so much fun. Nor do you want to keep telling them how much you miss them. You do that and they will begin to think, 'Hey, I should be there instead of here.'

"Another thing that is important for them is to know that things are the way they were when they left. If they have a car, they need to know that it is still in the garage and not being abused. They like to know that their room is unchanged and that you haven't rented it out or given it to a younger brother. They like to have that security and when they come home, they will spot anything that is different. For example when our son came home that first Thanksgiving, he had just stepped into the kitchen when he said, 'Mom! You've got new salt and pepper shakers!'

"Also, if there is a girl friend and you have a good open relationship with her, try to discourage her from writing and saying, 'Oh, I miss you so much,' or 'Gee, I wish you were here so we could do this or that.' They are lonely enough without the girlfriend making it worse."

Letters from home are important, but so are letters from other people. Several creative parents told of how they were able to generate such letters. One mother put a request on the church bulletin board along with the cadet's address. Another mother gave stamped, addressed envelopes to her son's coaches and close friends. Still another mother persuaded all of her cadet's uncles, aunts and cousins to write at least once during the first semester.

Some plebes offered this advice: "Even if you just print out a joke or an article to keep us in touch with the real world, it put's a smile on our face." Another agreed, "The mail you receive holds you — just one word is really nice, just to see that someone is thinking about you."

Note that during CBT, the envelopes will be "inspected" by the upperclass. If the letter comes in a white envelope, addressed in black ink, with a plain stamp, it will attract no special notice. If the letter is in a pink envelope with curly writing, the new cadet will receive some (joking) harassment and may even have to do some pushups. The plebes disagreed about whether this was to be avoided — said one, "For me, I'm happy to do pushups for a pink letter!"

After you have expended heroic efforts getting mail to your cadet, you and the other letter writers should not be disappointed when the letters are not answered. Why? Because the cadets are too busy. Almost every waking moment in their day is taken up with some activity — and many fall behind and have to use their weekends to catch up. Also, when the cadets do get a few spare moments, they should spend that time getting what they need the most: sleep! First-year cadets are always tired — so tired that they often have to stand up in class just to keep from falling asleep. So when you cajole uncles, aunts, cousins and friends to write your cadet, also explain why they are not likely to get their letters answered. Said a plebe, "Send letters, but don't expect a reply."

Another way to support your cadet is with packages of good things to eat and drink — packages that the cadets call "boodle boxes." Do not send boodle boxes during CBT, or "the cadre will confiscate them and eat them." But after Acceptance Day, treats are appreciated. Many parents gave detailed information on every aspect of sending boodle boxes. Here is a sampling of their comments.

Said the mother who has had two at West Point and one at Navy: "Lots of parents wonder why they need to send all that food to those kids. They don't realize that it isn't like an ordinary college with a 7-11 just down the street."

A mother from Rhode Island: "You must send boodle boxes--the other kids will be getting them and yours will feel left out if you don't. And when you send them, if you send one candy bar, send ten so everyone in the squad will have one. They all share so your cadet will be paid pack."

Several parents warned against sending a birthday cake the first year without consulting the cadet first. In some companies the new cadets or plebes do not dare drawn attention to themselves — to some upperclassmen, the "birthday boy or girl" is free game for whatever harassment they can dream up.

Said a mother from Rhode Island, "The mother may think she is doing a terrific thing when she sends a cake or flowers to a young lady, and she has no idea what the poor girl suffers because of it."

Every year parents receive information on local companies that will deliver treats to the cadets — things like fresh baked chocolate chip cookies and birthday cakes. The parents who use those companies said that they do a good job and they recommended them to other parents. One that is popular with cadets is called Cadets, Cakes and Cookies. Their web site is **www.cadetscakesandcookies.com** — you can order treats on line and have them delivered.

An indirect way you can support your cadet is to urge him or her to take advantage of the Sponsor Program. Sponsors, also called Mentors, are normally West Point officers who have volunteered to let cadets use their home as a place to relax and experience some of the pleasures of family life when the cadets have free time.

Many parents gave the sponsors rave reviews and were cited for doing many wonderful things. For example, some were praised for taking cadets to New York to catch planes home for Christmas when the public transportation system went haywire. Others were cited for visiting cadets in the hospital and keeping the parents informed with regular phone calls. Then there was a parent who told of his son who had made up his mind to resign after Christmas of his first year, but who was convinced to stay by his sponsor.

A small minority of the parents were not that enthusiastic about the sponsor program. Mostly they cited poor rapport between the cadet and mentor, and sponsors who were only mildly interested in the program.

So what can parents do when cadets do not have a good match? Urge your cadet to get a new sponsor if the first one does not work out satisfactorily. There are several ways to do that.

The official way is to go to the officer in charge of the program and ask for another one. One of the unofficial ways is for the cadet to ask a friend or roommate who has a good sponsor if he or she can tag along. Cadets and sponsors also find each other through good luck — maybe they strike a special relationship with a professor or coach and adopt one another.

Another unofficial procedure is to pick up a sponsor at one of the worship services. With each service there is a social period where, according to several parents, the chapel members look for cadets whom they can bring to their homes and for whom they can help ease the pangs of loneliness. Of the unofficial methods for obtaining a good mentor, the latter is highly recommended for the cadets who will be attending chapel anyway.

PARENTS' CLUBS AND PARENTS NET

Parents' clubs provide a variety of support services and social networks for parents of West Point cadets. Said one parent, "It's a big source of information, a support group for parents with no military experience."

Parents' clubs often host picnics or military balls to unite alumni, cadets, candidates, and their families. They may send cards and packages to cadets from their region. Most of all, they provide a way for parents of new cadets to connect with parents of upperclass cadets and graduates, so they can ask questions and seek advice.

To locate your parents' club, go to west-point.org/parent. If your parent's club does not have a web site, you will be linked to a public affairs representative who will give you contact information. The site also has links to other related sites.

One of those related sites is called West Point Parents Net, west-point.org/parent/wpp-net/. This site uses parent moderators to pass news and information to registered parents. The network also has chat groups, where you can get questions answered by parents of upperclass cadets or graduates.

DOWNER PHONE CALLS

The worst problem for most parents is the downer phone calls. All cadets have phones in their rooms, so calling home is easy. Typically, the cadet will call home after a few weeks or a few months in some state of frustration or exasperation. All the parents say that this is normal behavior and that a parent should expect calls like this. They point out that besides homesickness, the cadets are undergoing a traumatic change in their lifestyle.

Some get stressed by low grades — which few have ever seen during their previous twelve years of schooling. Parents who have lived through many such phone calls had a variety of advice. Here is a sampling:

A father from Florida: "His first calls were not really downers, but I suspected that when we got up there on Labor Day that he would need to unload — which he did. He was very quiet for the whole weekend but before we left I knew he wanted to talk. I said, 'What's wrong? You're not yourself.' He broke into tears and said, 'Dad, this is not a fun place to be. No matter how hard you try you can't control anything — no matter how hard you work you can't influence the situation.'

"I said — and I have a military background — 'Son, that is precisely how they want you to feel. As an Army officer you are not going to be able to control anything but yourself and the soldiers who are, hopefully, trained and disciplined to do what you command. You can't control artillery, air, supplies — and you certainly can't control the enemy.' I think that talk helped; it is important for cadets to understand why they being treated as they are."

A mother and parents' club president from Pennsylvania: "I had those calls and I hear about them all the time. I tell those I counsel to assess the day of the week and the time of day they are calling. Sometimes you find out that the downer calls may coincide with a bad day. My son used to always call on Tuesday evening about eight o'clock. He would be very down, but by the end of the conversation he would get everything out of his system and he would be fine — although we would worry until the next call. We found out later that Tuesday was a long, hard day for him. He was in an advanced scuba diving class, which he practiced the first thing in the morning, then he had classes all day and hockey afterwards. By eight o'clock, still facing hours of homework, he just wasn't himself — he was exhausted. The Sunday calls were nothing like that — on Sundays he had a whole different outlook on life.

"What do you say if they hate it so much they want to quit? It depends upon the kid, of course, but, generally, I advise parents to try and get them to finish the year — to give it a fair trial. In fact, I see nothing wrong with a parent arguing strenuously when they believe the kid has not given it a fair trial — at least through the first semester.

"However, if the kid insists on coming home, I think at least one of the parents, if possible, should go there and talk everything over — don't just let them quit without talking them through all their options. I always stress the importance of letting them know that you won't be disappointed in them if they quit — they need to know that they have the complete support of the parents. Many times I think they just need a chance to unload and to talk things out. The worst thing is when the parents get upset and act like it is the end of the world when the kid wants to quit."

A mother from Illinois put the ups and downs this way: "When we would get one of those calls, my husband would talk briefly, then the other son would talk because he was always positive and encouraging. Then, when I picked up the phone, I could hear the change in voice — he just wanted to get out all his misery to me. And I would listen and just mother him to death over the phone — I'd just let him be miserable.

"Later we found out that the pattern of the downer calls was related to the sleep that he got — the more tired and worn down he got, the more down he would be. Also, if he was in the process of doing something he really hated, he would be down. I remember how he was not thrilled with the boxing — he didn't like his nose bleeding every time — that got him down. But now he is fine. He is 38th in his class and is on the regimental staff."

A father and former parents' club president from Illinois: "One of the worst problems I have seen is when kids get low grades and the parents refuse to accept that. It is hard when they have high SATs and are used to getting good grades in high school. Parents have to realize that it is much harder at West Point and that high grades in high school don't necessarily mean a thing. If parents will accept those low grades as normal, at least for awhile, then they can counsel the cadet and encourage him"

A mother and parents' club president from Kansas: "They're up and down and you just have to expect that. The important thing is to listen but not sympathize — I mean don't side with them against West Point. I think kids who have always had it good are the ones it is hardest on. Those who have been slapped around by life are more likely to rebound when they're low."

A mother from California: "Almost all of them hate it at first and they call home really down. I think you have to encourage them and tell them to just hang in there another week or until Thanksgiving or until Christmas. Keep telling them that it will get easier. I say this because my son would be down one week because things were miserable and I would get off the phone and worry all week. Then, the next week he calls and says, 'Oh mom, you know what happened? I was voted plebe of the week.' So it is up and down, and it goes like that.

"I think the key is to always talk positive — be upbeat, without offending them, of course."

Said two parents from Texas, both with graduate degrees in psychology: "You have to be a good listener but what do you say? We used a counselor's technique which is basically to repeat what he is saying. 'That math is really hard, huh? So it's really cold and dreary up there.' Just repeat their problems. What they want is for you to understand what they are going through. By repeating what they are saying, you are convincing them that you do understand."

An Ohio mother: "Our son wanted West Point from the time he knew what it was, but after two weeks there, we got the first call and he said he was thinking of bagging it. Luckily we have been a family that always communicated so we had some good long talks. The most important thing in these talks is to lead the kid back through the reasons why he wanted it in the first place, then ask if there has been any change in goals. I think you have to be sympathetic but also strong in insisting that they give it the chance that it needs.

"Part of the problem is that they are all bright kids and they try to make logic out of situations that are not logical. They can't accept things at face value — they can't accept standard answers without questioning them. They just have to realize that they must obey without questioning.

"That is a real hard adjustment and a lot of them go through the first few months doubting whether they made the right decision. Parents have to gather together their inner strength and somehow convince them that they did make they right decision — support them long enough so the cadet himself can make a decision based on intelligence rather than emotion and two or three weeks without sleep."

A Virginia parent: "Sometimes he just needed a sounding board. He always asked for dad, who would say to hang in there. It's natural. They get frustrated over not doing well. They're used to being Big Men on Campus, they're competitive. Just let them know you're proud. Try to give them perspective, let them know how well they've been doing, that time is passing, and it will get easier."

PARENT VISITS

One of the best ways to support cadets is to visit them.

The parents who commented on these visits had mixed feelings about them. Some believed that such visits helped their cadets while others felt that the visit was too short to be worthwhile or that seeing the family for such a brief time was tantalizing and only increased the cadet's anxiety. An Academy official who is a graduate and whose son is a graduate discouraged frequent visits of this type. His main concern was parents who try to remain overly involved in the cadet's life. "Hovering parents," he said, "cause the plebes to have great turmoil."

The first good opportunity to visit cadets is during Acceptance Day Weekend, when your son or daughter completes Cadet Basic Training and is officially accepted into the Corps of Cadets. Your cadet will be very proud of this accomplishment, and may want to share it with you. A word of warning from one cadet: "Your parents will expect you to be free the whole time, but you still have to do the parade and an inspection. So they may have to wait awhile" before spending time together.

Said a plebe, "Come [to Acceptance Day] if you can. They've accomplished such a large goal. It's a big morale booster to have some contact" with family.

Parents strongly believe that a visit at this time can be very beneficial to the cadet. They also gave several specific recommendations, including this very important one: get your room reservations the same day your cadet accepts the appointment. An on-line search will reveal plenty of options, but realize that if you book late, you can easily end up 45 minutes away. That takes time away from your cadet and fun activities you would rather do. Some stay in RV parks to avoid the hotel issue.

Most parents, and all cadets, would advise you to visit on Parents Weekend at just about any cost.

United States Military Academy

Other recommendations:

A father and parents' club president from Florida: "Be prepared for a shock if you go up there Labor Day Weekend. Our son had lost fifteen pounds and that stupid cover on his head was too big and sitting down on his ears. We have a snapshot of me standing by him and I don't even recognize him. There is no need to worry, though. They monitor the cadets' weight and they will gain it back. But there is a real need for them to have things like peanut butter and jelly to take back to their room."

A father from Michigan: "You have to go there realizing that your cadet may get put on restriction or may have duty sometime during the three days. It is a good idea to have him [or her] call before you leave home."

"One thing to remember, if you go up there for that Labor Day Weekend — don't go with any preconceived notions of what you are going to do [other than a picnic]. Let the cadet decide what to do. Some are more adventurous than others and they will approach their mother and give her a kiss or give their father a hug — but they're told they can't display affection in public so they may not do this. Just be ready to react to their wants and needs — and realize that you may spend a lot of time just watching them sleep.

A mother from Kansas had other suggestions for things to bring: "This is the time to build their morale. Bring surprise letters that they can take back to their room and read. Bring things from home, like a leaf of mint from the back yard or pictures of the dog. Then, when you are ready to leave, hand them an envelope with two or three tickets for Sunday brunch at the Hotel Thayer. Later, when your cadet has the opportunity, he or she can take one or two friends and they can enjoy a wonderful meal."

A mother from Rhode Island cautioned parents not to be inquisitive when they visit their cadet. She said: "I think one of the biggest mistakes parents make is when they begin pumping the kid for information. I know, it's natural to be curious — you want to know what they are going through and how they are doing. But just try to remember what you feel like after a hard day, when everything is very difficult and things have gone wrong. Do you want to come home and begin talking about it? My advice is to relax and simply enjoy your cadet, and if he wants to bring up something and talk about it, let him do it. And remember, the system they're in makes them feel like they are not doing well — so don't ask how they are doing or if they like it. If they are truthful, they will have to say negative things. So just let them lead the discussions."

Football game weekends are also popular times for family visits. Your cadet will have to attend the football game, and you will probably enjoy the festivities as well. Plan ahead. Warned one parent, "The hotel situation is dreadful. Get a reservation months ahead of time if you want to be even close. It took an hour to get in the gate for the Army Air Force game."Said a plebe, "Come any time you can. It's always good to see friends and family." Agreed another, "My mom comes up every few months, especially now during the gloom period [the cold, dark winter months between the holidays and spring break], just to give me a break."

PLEBE PARENT WEEKEND

The timing of Plebe Parent Weekend has been changing almost year to year — from the fall to right before spring break and back again. For parents who want to know as soon as possible when it will be, keep checking the West Point web page, **www.usma.edu**.

Whenever it occurs, all the parents who were interviewed strongly urged other parents not to miss Plebe Parent Weekend.

Said a mother from Minnesota: "We would do it again even if we had to take a second mortgage on our house — it is so important for your cadet. We took seven other children when we went — the airline had a promotion where kids under 16 could fly free — and we rented two cars. The kids still talk about that weekend — they had so much fun. I could write a book about the whole weekend. I'm so glad we didn't miss it."

A father and retired colonel from Rhode Island: "I strongly recommend it. There are no upperclassmen around, you get to tour everything, eat in the mess hall — it gives the parents a very good sense of what West Point is. Also it gives the cadets a chance to show the parents everything — their rooms — we even toured the kitchens as insiders."

A mother and parents' club president from Pennsylvania: "I think it is very important, especially on the Friday when the barracks are open and when the Tac Officer[2] meets each individual parent. You get to know how the Tac feels about your cadet and he [or she] gets a feel for what the cadet has at home. And of all the tours, I would say don't miss the tour of the Superintendent's home — you have to get tickets for it. Also, I found the kitchens and the tailor shops very interesting."

Other parents had specific recommendations regarding Plebe Parent Weekend.

A mother from California: "Be sure and take warm clothes — we tend to forget things like that living in Southern California. It can be very cold up there."

A mother from Pennsylvania: "Take good walking shoes because you are going to be doing a lot of it. For clothing, plan on casual clothes during the day — afternoon clothes are fine for touring the Superintendent's house. However, they have a formal dinner and military ball, and while you see men in suits as well as formal attire, the formal wear looks very elegant. It was interesting to me to see all the clothes and you could almost tell what region people came from — for example, the Southern girls wore lovely full gowns with crinolines and hooped skirts."

An upperclass cadet also encouraged parents to come to Plebe Parent Weekend if at all possible: "Make sure you come. Plebes get to run the place. You can step outside what you're going through and just feel proud."

Parents spoke of two potential problems associated with Plebe Parent Weekend. One is housing, and they strongly recommend that parents get their reservations as soon as possible.

The other problem, for some parents, is a girlfriend problem.

The question that troubles parents is: Should we or should we not take the girlfriend along? (None of the parents mentioned a boyfriend problem.)

Numerous parents commented on the problem and their feelings and experiences were varied. The majority definitely believed that the girlfriend should be left home so the cadet would not be torn between her and the family. They cited the need of the cadet to relax and be nurtured, and not to have additional pressure. However, many qualified this recommendation by saying that if the visit by the girlfriend is really important to the cadet, by all means take her along. The bottom line is the cadet's happiness.

---

[2] The Tac Officer, or Tactical Officer, is the officer in command of each company of about 120 cadets. They are typically majors with several tours of duty under their belts. While the upperclass cadets are responsible for day-to-day operations in their company, the Tac Officers provide guidance and supervision.

A few of the parents described good experiences when they took the girlfriend along, but they qualified their comments with such statements as: "She was a jewel," and "She was like a part of the family and very supportive of what he was doing."

OTHER ADVICE

Several parents commented about their cadets' attitude and behavior during vacations at home. They advised not to expect a transformation in the way the cadets keep their room. They say that the typical parent expects the West Point standards to rub off and that the cadets will keep their rooms neat and orderly. Instead, the parents say the cadets often regress and are as bad or worse than when they left — that they overreact to what they have been through.

They will want to forget about West Point completely for awhile. An upperclass cadet complained that her parents had redecorated her room with West Point memorabilia. "When we come home, we want things the same as they were. And don't expect us to wear a uniform when we're home."

Another problem at vacation time is that the cadets come home, sleep for a day and a half, then venture off and spend more time with their friends than with their family. Parents complained of various degrees of disappointment about this behavior, but all acknowledged that visits with friends ended up having positive value because the cadets see just how much more they, themselves, have matured as compared to their friends.

Parents also cautioned not to plan things for the vacationing cadet, especially visits to Uncle Joe and Aunt Millie in full dress uniform! A family picture is okay, they say, but otherwise the advice is to let the cadet sleep, eat lots of whatever they crave, let them zonk on television if they desire, and, in general, keep the vacations as low key as possible.

Cadets become much closer to their roommates and classmates than at civilian colleges so don't be surprised, say parents, when your cadet wants to bring friends home during a vacation. Also, they say that parents should not be disappointed when the cadets announce that they are going to spend their vacation at their friend's home or do some traveling with their friends. Just try to remember that it is those friends who have sustained your cadet and shared long periods of adversity. So it is perfectly natural for them to also want to share some of the good times with their friends.

Any calls concerning their cadet's welfare should be directed to the Company Tactical Officer. However, the cadets themselves almost begged the author to advise parents not to call the Tac unless it was something critically important. Plebes, especially, do not want to draw attention to themselves, and they worry that knowledge of a call from a parent will get around their Company and they will somehow suffer from it

Said one cadet, "Don't ever call the Tac or the Superintendent. Just don't get involved. We're not in middle school anymore. It makes [the cadet] look like an idiot, and the cadre will make fun."

But, by all means, if there is an emergency, or if the parent really feels that a cadet is having some kind of threatening problem, call the Tac. And, if you are not satisfied with what the Tac is doing or has told you, you are perfectly within your right to move up the chain of command; after the Tac, call the Regimental Tactical Officer (RTO), and if still not satisfied, call the Brigade Tactical Officer (BTO). You can get those numbers from the West Point switchboard: 914-938-4011.

An alternative to contacting the Tac is to contact one of the chaplains. They have the ability to check out a number of problems without consulting the Tac or anyone else, and at certain times, like when the cadet is in the hospital, they can be a very good source of help. They are especially helpful in handling sensitive matters such as family problems that parents want to keep confidential. To contact a chaplain, just call the switchboard — they are on call 24-hours a day.

We began this chapter talking about money — and the fact that West Point parents do not have the burden of college tuition. But will your cadet need spending money? The answer depends on whom you ask. Said one man, "The first year, you may need money for plane tickets. Otherwise, you should be able to live on your pay." A plebe echoed this thought, "They provide almost everything you need. Your pay is probably enough." Another cadet, who is an intercollegiate athlete, countered, "If you're in sports, it can get expensive. You end up paying for food, and some fees." Another suggested, "Send quarters for laundry."

Several cadets recommended applying for scholarships, even once an appointment has been received and accepted. Those small scholarships, say $500 or $1000, can provide money for eating out and traveling the entire plebe year.

Graduation day will be one of the most memorable for you and your cadet. Remember that everyone at West Point is there to help them finish successfully. *United States Military Academy*

A final bit of advice from the authors (and several cadets we interviewed). Don't worry! That is easier said than done, we realize. But if your son or daughter was good enough to get an appointment to West Point, he or she is good enough to succeed there. Their success will come to them through heartache, frustration, and failure. Be ready for that. But realize that thousands of other parents' sons and daughters before them have survived the experience.

You will have a unique opportunity to witness their transformation from wide-eyed high school kid to self-assured Army officer. Take credit for the character and values you gave them, and enjoy being proud of your West Point cadet.

Index

Acknowledgements

All four editions of this book are the result of hundreds of people who were willing to help future cadets find their way. We can't name them all, but to all the administrators, professors, cadets, congressional staffers and panelists, liaison officers, and parents who offered us their time and insights: Thank you.

We can acknowledge a few special individuals who were especially helpful. Above all, we thank Mr. Frank DeMaro of USMA Public Affairs. We were so fortunate, after working with him on the third edition, to find him still there, and of course he was once again so amazingly helpful. We really couldn't do it without him.

We want to thank Major Aaron Barreda in Military Training, Colonel (Father) Matt Pawlikowski, Dr. Jeffrey D. Peterson from the Simon Center for the Professional Military Ethic, Dr. (Professor) Rasheed Hosein with the Muslim Club, Lieutenant Colonel Timothy Viles in Admissions, Colonel John Hartke in the Physics Department, and Lieutenant Tony Zupancic in the English Department. Your guidance and insights were superb.

Most important, we want to thank the cadets and graduates who shared their advice and perspectives, successes and failures — all with great honestly and humility. Though we cannot list you all by name, we value your stories and insights as you let us share in your experiences, and we admire you for your service and achievements.

A few final thank yous from Sue Ross: I have learned so much from Bill Smallwood, the author of the first two editions of this book. His passion for helping young men and women find their path to success is the driving force behind this work. Thanks to Bill and his wife, Patricia, for allowing me to take over this project. And to Lieutenant Colonel (retired) Randy Lee, you are not only a great source of inside information and contacts, but also a wise adviser and a source of many laughs. It was a pleasure to work with you once again.